"I really like how this book is broken [...] and easy-to-read chapters. The perso[...] me and help me know I am not alon[...] I get married to have sex."                    —Tom, 15-year-old

"It is almost impossible to read this and not feel good about yourself. From reading this book, I feel that no matter what anybody says or does I'M WORTH WAITING FOR! You know God loves YOU. So, it's no longer just a mantra that pops in your head when you're at a weak point—it's a standard of living you'll want to set for yourself. This book should be essential for every teenager."                    —Jessica, 17-year-old

"Before I read this book, I didn't know if I wanted to live a chaste life. But once I started reading the book, it became clear to me how awesome living a chaste life actually is. This book inspired me to make the right decision." —Nikki, 14-year-old

"I always assumed I would live chastely, always giving a casual 'Yes' if ever asked if I did. Now that I have read *A Case for Chastity*, I understand that living chastity is the way to live my life to the fullest."                    —Bo, 18-year-old

"As a mother, I am grateful for this book because I now have plenty of positive analogies to help my children embrace chastity instead of using scare tactics to keep my kids away from sex."                    —Beth, parent

"As the father of a teenage son and two daughters, I appreciate the recognition that chastity presents different issues for each gender. The real-life testimonials perfectly underline what an emotional and spiritual dead end promiscuity is and the lasting fulfillment that follows from chastity."    —David, parent

*A Case for*
# CHASTITY

# A Case for
# CHASTITY

• • • • • • • • • • • • • • • • • • • • • • • • • • • • • •

## THE WAY TO REAL LOVE
## AND TRUE FREEDOM
## FOR CATHOLIC TEENS

An A to Z Guide

HEATHER GALLAGHER and PETER VLAHUTIN

Liguori
LIGUORI, MISSOURI

*Imprimi Potest:*
Richard Thibodeau, C.Ss.R.
Provincial, Denver Province
The Redemptorists

*Imprimatur:*
Most Reverend Robert J. Hermann
Auxiliary Bishop of St. Louis

Published by Liguori Publications
Liguori, Missouri
www.liguori.org

Library of Congress Catalog Control Number: 2003113695
ISBN 0-7648-1102-9
Copyright 2003 by Heather Gallagher and Peter Vlahutin

Printed in the United States of America
08 07 06 05 04   6 5 4 3 2

# CONTENTS

· · · · · · · · · · ·

*Dedicated to John Paul Thomas Vlahutin.*
*Miracles happen.*
*Your life is living proof.*
*May God bless you throughout all of life*
*as much as he has in your first four months.*

Love, and do what you will.
SAINT AUGUSTINE OF HIPPO

How do I love thee? Let me count the ways.
I love thee to the depth and breadth and height
My soul can reach, when feeling out of sight
For the ends of Being and ideal Grace.
I love thee to the level of everyday's
Most quiet need, by sun and candle-light.
I love thee freely, as men strive for Right;
I love thee purely, as they turn from Praise.
I love thee with the passion put to use
In my old griefs, and with my childhood's faith.
I love thee with a love I seemed to lose
With my lost saints, — I love thee with the breath,
Smiles, tears, of all my life! — and, if God choose,
I shall but love thee better after death.

*SONNET XLIII*, ELIZABETH BARRETT BROWNING

As an apple tree among the trees of the wood, so is my beloved among young men. With great delight I sat in his shadow, and his fruit was sweet to my taste. He brought me to the banqueting house, and his intention toward me was love.

SONG OF SONGS 2:3–4

# ACKNOWLEDGMENTS

. . . . . . . . . . .

First of all, we want to express our gratitude to Jesus, our inspiration, joy, and strength. Thank you to the Holy Spirit who never left our side.

Second, we want to thank our dear friends and family members for the many prayers and words of encouragement. A special thanks goes out to our prayer community, the charismatic orthodox Catholics of God's Gang, The REAP Team, NET Ministries, and our own men's and women's prayer groups who continue to love, challenge, and form both of us.

Most especially, thank you to all those who have edited and contributed: Bob and Meredith Bennett, Mary Allhoff, Bo Purcell, Jessica Bollasina, Nikki Reinkemeyer, Beth Vortriede, Thomas Vortriede, Aggie Gallagher, Kelley Basta, Dianne Guittar, Stacey Chik, Julie Fague, Jamie Klemmer, and Jen Sallwasser. Much thanks to the youth groups who contributed to specific chapters: SALLT, God's Gang, and Our Lady of the Pillar. Similar thanks to all of Mr. Pat Tinkham's sophomore and junior religion classes at Chaminade College Preparatory School who read chapters and provided feedback.

Praise be to God for all those who have specifically encouraged us: Monsignor Francis Kelley of the Archdiocese of Boston and the Most Reverend Archbishop Timothy Dolan of the Archdiocese of Milwaukee.

Thanks also to all the people at Liguori Publications who helped everything come together: Judy, John, Bob, Jodi, Pam, Barb, Cecelia, and everyone else who had a hand in this project. We would also like to thank Steve Givens for getting us in touch with Liguori.

• • •

*From Heather:* I want to especially thank my incredibly faith-filled and supportive parents who literally took me in during this project. Without your unconditional love and unfailing enthusiasm, I wouldn't know where I was or where I was heading. Your witness has given me a solid foundation and compass to get wherever God leads me. And, thanks to Paul Masek for putting up with me and my wacky schedule while finishing this project. I couldn't imagine a more wonderful boss. To all the teens I have met and continue to work with in ministry, who bless me every day, thanks for being my inspiration and filling my life with abundant joy.

*From Pete:* This project could not have happened without the consent and support of my loving wife, Jenny. Thank you for all your encouragement and for the many sacrifices you've made to give me this opportunity. More importantly, thank you for making your own choice for chastity and for blessing me and our marriage with that decision. A big thanks also to Chaminade and the wonderfully supportive staff and students.

• • •

Last, but not least, thanks to all the people whose stories are shared within these pages. Your lives have inspired us. We pray your stories will shed light upon the truth and guide many others to the choice of chastity.

# INTRODUCTION

· · · · · · · · · · · ·

## Why Should I Read This Book?

Movies, television programs, advertisements, and music bombard teens with hundreds of sexual messages every day. These messages say: "Sex is fun," "Experimenting sexually is part of growing up," "Everyone is doing it," "Being in love or having an attraction means having sex," "Use protection and you'll be safe," "If you want it, you can have it," and many similar thoughts that encourage and promote premarital sexual activity. The media must make money and therefore doesn't care if you ever achieve lasting loving relationships. Most moviemakers and musicians don't care if you find true and lasting freedom in your life.

Some people who do seem to care, however, often send confusing messages. Some want to provide particular sexual information and even contraception—condoms and birth-control pills—to teens to help them "mature" sexually. Others attempt to scare teenagers into abstinence, focusing only on sexually transmitted diseases (STDs) or pregnancy. Some even condemn sex and teens who consider enjoying it with the messages, "Sex is bad" or "Just say no!"

There is another side to the story, another message that is worth listening to. This alternate message actually elevates above the extremes of careless sexual liberation and frigid sexual repression. It recognizes and respects the importance, value, and power of sex. It claims that there is a purpose to our sexuality and that when we fulfill that purpose, we experience the best that life has to offer. It is the message of respect for oneself, one's sexuality, and one's relationships; it is the message of chastity.

Simply put, chastity views and treats sex and sexuality in all people with complete respect and love, nothing less. Chastity is the virtue that elevates our sexuality to such a place of importance that we would only express sexual acts in the context of marriage.

We, Heather and Pete, have accepted this message and live it. In our work with young people, we have met thousands of teenagers who have chosen this message of chastity over the sex-crazed message of popular culture. In choosing chastity, we have found true freedom and the ability to give and experience real love. More importantly, we believe that this message is not only for us, but that all people who choose chastity can find the same freedom and the same love.

This book is not about STD statistics or scaring teens to say "no" to sex. Rather, it is about presenting a case for chastity so teens have enough knowledge and wisdom to confidently choose a "yes" for chastity. Although there is validity in exposing the many medical, physical dangers of promiscuous sex, we are leaving that task to others. We choose to shed light on the often unspoken yet extremely powerful effects of sex on one's intellectual, emotional, and spiritual health—how we're internally shaped by our sexual choices.

## What's This?

Throughout this book, you will see text inserts, such as this, at various points in the chapters. In these sections, you will find the stories of real people. Most names have been changed because of the personal nature of the stories. These stories support the points we are making and show how our understanding—yours and ours—of our sexuality is often shaped by real-life experiences.

On the following pages, you will read our case, our argument, for the virtue of chastity. If you don't know much about chastity or about the Catholic Church's teachings on sexuality, it may sound foreign or strange to you. Be patient, listen carefully, and hear us out. The message we are sharing is not our own; it is the message of our sexuality as God intended it. It comes from his Word and the teachings of his Church. Even more relevant, however, is that it comes from our own lived experiences and the experiences of many people that we know. These lived experiences are our evidence.

> After presenting the topic of chastity to a group of ninth-grade students, one student approached us and said, "You were here two years ago and talked about chastity then, too. I tore up the chastity commitment cards you passed out. I thought, 'I'm going to do whatever I want with my body.' However, I started looking around at my friends and other teens in these past two years, and I know exactly why this chastity commitment makes sense now. All I needed was a dose of real life. Can I have another card?"

Papal Household preacher, Capuchin Father Raniero Cantalamessa said, "It is a duty and a joy for believers to rediscover the radical alternative of the Gospel: chastity. This alternative does not disqualify or blame sex, as opposed to what the secular press says. On the contrary, it emphasizes its human, free, and rational character."[1]

You are the judges, and your own life is the proving ground. You can blindly accept the sexual messages of the mass media, or you can decide which makes more sense for your life. At the very least, you owe it to yourself to listen to, and consider, what God might have to say. We promise you that if you wholeheartedly choose this approach, if you choose chastity for a lifetime, you will not be left sexually unsatisfied or disappointed.

We, Heather and Pete, are average people. We are young adults who grew up in the 1980s and the 1990s. Heather is from the Midwest, has lived in Ireland, and traveled to Australia and throughout Europe. She is a football and basketball fanatic and loves to dance.

Pete grew up in the West, attended high school in the East, and has settled in the Midwest; he is into sports, plays the guitar, and likes listening to music and watching movies. Both of us have seen the effects of the choices we and our friends have made. When it comes to conclusions about sex, we have found tremendous insight from sharing what has happened to couples we know. You deserve to benefit from this insight as well. We want you to know this message and to experience what it can mean for your life.

The approach to sex presented in this book is not one of those pie-in-the-sky ideals that isn't applicable to anyone's life. It isn't some theory that hasn't been put into practice successfully either. And it especially is not something that we aren't also trying to live out ourselves. Heather, a single young adult, is living out this message. Pete, a married young adult, is living out this message. By the time you finish this book, we hope that you are living the message as well.

## Authors' Note

1. Though we refer to marriage as a future event, we know that not everyone reading this book will be called to marriage. It is our hope that some of you will pursue priesthood and religious life. It would be awkward for us to always tack on to the end of every reference to marriage the phrase "if you're called to marriage." However, know that this is our assumption.

2. Writers and speakers in our culture often refer to men and women as the "opposite sex," pairing off the two sexes in opposition to each other. We will use the term "complementary sex" for this idea. Men and women complement each other—sexually and in other ways—so we prefer this term as a more accurate one.

3. A great deal of recent political discussion has focused on the nature of marriage. In this book, marriage means the union of a man and a woman as husband and wife. Anything else that pretends to be marriage is not marriage as we are presenting it here.

# ATTITUDES
# AND APPROACHES
· · · · · · · · · · ·

## What Choices Do I Have?

Good news: you have a choice. Despite external pressures from friends, family, teachers, peers, Hollywood, and even society as a whole, God has given you free will to choose your own path in life. This freedom gives us tremendous power.

God doesn't directly prevent us from choosing wrong or harmful things, not even where sexuality is concerned. God isn't some police officer in the sky, waiting for people to mess up so he can banish them to hell.

Even if you have had only casual conversation about sex with class-mates and friends, you know that human beings take different approaches toward their own sexuality. While not an exhaustive list, the approaches that follow include the general attitudes toward sex that exist among the many people in our culture, especially among teenagers.

*Sex: An Extracurricular Activity:* This approach can be summed up in three words: Sex is fun! Since life is all about having fun (as long as no one is seriously hurt), teens should have as much fun in life while they can, and this search includes that super-fun activity of sex.

*Sex in a Committed Relationship:* A second approach involves sex only in a committed relationship. The level of commitment can vary, but it is understood that one doesn't have sex with just anyone. Usu-ally, this approach involves a dating relationship.

1

*In Love, Sex Is OK:* Those who subscribe to this third approach say that sex is acceptable as long as the couple is in love. These people tend not to have sex in every dating relationship, but they might engage in sex in every serious relationship.

*Sex to Gain Love:* Some people have experienced a lot of pain and hurt in their lives. Regardless of the source of pain and hurt, some people only feel loved and cherished when they are being held sexually. These people choose sex simply because it makes them feel loved. This response may seem to be a desperate way to act, but the majority of people in this category are probably unaware of the reasons why they are acting this way.

*Sex When I'm Ready:* This approach says that sex is OK when each of the people in the relationship is ready to have sex. For some, this approach refers to a certain comfort level in the relationship. For others, this approach refers to their own maturity level. For others, it may simply be when they feel ready to handle the consequences of having sex and are willing to take personal responsibility for their actions.

*Sex With That Special Someone:* Some people think that sex is very important and should be saved for that special someone. When that special someone comes along, they will instinctively know that this is the right person.

*Experience Is My Guide:* This approach says that part of the journey to maturity is discovering for oneself what is right and wrong, especially when it comes to sex. It says teens should experience as much as possible so that they can truly know who they are, what they like, and what they are good at. People adopting this approach believe experience is critical for growth and for the ability to please one's spouse when one gets married.

*Sex Without Intercourse:* Some people really want to save sexual intercourse for marriage. However, one can do a lot sexually without "going all the way." These people attempt to free themselves from the physical consequences of intercourse yet still allow themselves the pleasures that come from relating to another sexually.

*Sex As Increased Affection:* For these people, every relationship must be more intimate than the previous relationship. If one is in enough relationships, eventually sex will need to be involved.

*Sex Just Happened:* Unfortunately, this unintended approach happens to too many teens. They find themselves in a situation where things start happening, and before they realize it, they've had sex.

*Abstinence Only:* This approach says that sex is WRONG! and that everyone should abstain from sexual activity until married. Abstinence is all about not having sex. Some teenagers are choosing this approach for themselves, but frequently this course of action is one presented to teens by adults.

*Sex: A Necessary Evil:* Simply put, this approach says sex is a necessary evil. It is necessary for conceiving children, but by nature sex is an evil act. People adopting this approach usually equate sex with lust, guilt, or shame—so much so that they cannot engage in any act of sex, married or otherwise, without thinking they are sinning.

*I Determine What It Means:* The final approach we will address is a slight variation on the above attitudes. In this approach, the individual says, "I, and only I, can determine what sex means. If I want it to be for love, then it can be for love. If I want it to be for fun, then it can be for fun." People who take this approach can move from sexual experience to sexual experience and determine the meaning of sex in each context. Some who adopt this approach can be very faithful when in a committed relationship; they can also be very promiscuous when not in a relationship and are using sex simply for fun.

In our work with teenagers, we have been saddened by the number of teens who fall into the previously listed mentalities and the trap of misusing their sexuality. Those who have regretted past decisions and those who are currently involved in sexual relationships have given any number of reasons for their actions. Perhaps your friends or acquaintances—or even you—have used these reasons stated previously as a justification.

## It's Important to Choose

Occasionally, teens feel as if they can make a decision about their sexuality at a later date. For many of these teens, the moment when they need to implement the decision comes before they actually have made a considered choice. It is important to make a decision before you get in a situation that requires it.

Corey writes: Before my sophomore year in high school, I toured Europe with a group of the best high-school and college-aged musicians from my state. On this trip, I met a girl named Maria, who was absolutely drop-dead gorgeous. We spent a lot of time together on the trip and also after we got home. After school started, we didn't see each other as much but still kept in touch. After that school year—the summer before my junior year—we got back together. I realized then that when it came to sex, she was way, way more experienced than I was—meaning I was a virgin and she was not.

One weekday afternoon I went to her house when her parents were gone, and things got pretty hot pretty fast. No girl had ever treated me this way. In a moment of weakness, I was more than willing to give myself to her. We had sex—just one time, nothing special, no romantic do-it-all-night-long type of thing. A few minutes later she looked at a clock and just said, "Well, I have to go to dance class now. Call me tonight?"

On the way home, the shame shook me to the core. I was too numb to cry. I don't even remember the drive home. My next memory was Mom, smiling at me, asking me about how my afternoon went. The guilt and embarrassment I felt at that moment was indescribable. I couldn't look Mom in the eye—and it would be a while before I could look Dad, my brother, or my little sister in the eye either. I had always pictured talking about how I had sex with some girl with my friends and having them tell me how cool I was. In reality, I didn't tell a soul, since it was nothing to be proud of. It was just a waste of virginity on a girl I didn't even like enough to officially "go out with." I didn't tell any of my friends for weeks. I finally told my friend Tom one day because I thought I would explode, not because he'd think I was cool.

I have never felt so far removed from God in my entire life. He gave me a gift of sexuality and I had squandered it away on a weekday afternoon with some girl I never spoke more than two words to again. As the event faded into the past, I made no effort to resolve it. I just suppressed it so that I could keep the moral and spiritual questions at bay. The reality of what happened finally began to sink in. I wasn't expecting to have sex that day. I didn't have protection. What if she had gotten pregnant? She wasn't a virgin; what if I caught something? What would people think? I beat myself up, thinking that I was one of those bad kids

- whose world revolves around getting with as many girls as pos-
- sible. People who knew would think less of me; and that would
- make me a complete, total, and utter failure.

## The Danger of Choice

Making decisions is very difficult for some people and easy for others. Some people fall in between these extremes. Regardless of one's decision-making tendencies, the number of options to consider when it comes to using one's sexuality is mind numbing. A person might ask: How can I maximize my pleasure and minimize my pain and hurt? How can I truly get the most out of life and relationships without settling for less than the best?

The problem with making choices is that they become our choices, and we have to experience the consequences of those choices. When it comes to sex and sexuality, a number of people are making poor decisions. We don't believe that teenagers are so unintelligent and gullible that they are intentionally choosing less. Rather, the path that leads to real love and true freedom has probably not been shared with them in a way that makes sense and that they can understand. This path is chastity.

We believe that the best love, freedom, and sex cannot be found in any of the previously listed approaches. If you are interested in the best that life has to offer, keep on reading as we explain the approach of chastity, how it is different from these other attitudes, and how fulfilling this virtue can be in our lives and relationships.

# BE DIFFERENT

## But Everybody Else Is Doing It

Heather shares the following story:

The night after my college roommate lost her virginity the girls came rushing into our room to celebrate. Beth and her boyfriend had been dating for years; therefore, most agreed, "It's about time!" After Beth described some details, everyone in the room started sharing their first times. Two had lost their virginity with long-term boyfriends, another in the back seat of a car with a guy she never wanted to see again, and then it was my turn. Though I wasn't part of the "club," I shared my most romantic experience.

Ryan and I had been friends for months, talking on the phone for several hours every night. We shared so much with each other and connected on many levels. We were also very attracted to each other. One summer night, he showed up at my house. It was late, so we escaped to a nearby park and walked through the woods together. He was so sweet in the way that he treated me—with total respect. We didn't even kiss that night, but we held hands for the first time, embraced each other tightly, and experienced the beauty of being close to someone you care for deeply. The room went silent when I finished describing all the fun and romantic aspects of that night. One friend looked at me and asked, "Heather, why is your story so much better than ours?"

With so many sexual approaches available to us, we must decide what we desire most, for the present and the future. Many of the widely accepted attitudes about sex, such as those held by the young, trendy characters on most TV shows, give us little of what we need most: meaningful and deep relationships. Although such easily-entered-into sexual relationships might seem fun or loving at the time they are initiated, they frequently become shallow or emotionally painful. Many young people are finally asking: "Is there anything better out there?" "Do relationships with depth, passion, and true love actually exist?" Yes, but only if you rebel against culture and choose something radical for the twenty-first century—living virtuously. You might remember virtues from religion class: patience, compassion, kindness, humility, and the like. They not only still exist but they also elevate you above mediocrity.

You might be thinking, "But virtues aren't cool." That's because so few of us use them fully or regularly. Virtues are like muscles discovered when trying something new. When first snowboarding, I used muscles I never knew existed. Not only did using and developing these muscles improve my snowboarding skills and my fun, in the end I benefited because these muscles were exercised.

In a just-do-it culture, we easily forget about virtues, especially patience. We toss it out the window for instant results. We want everything right now. Some of us even fuss if fast food takes more than five minutes. Where sex is concerned, it seems like no one is waiting for marriage. As long as no one seems harmed, why should we be patient? Honestly, we don't need to exercise patience if all we desire in life is short-term thrills. However, short-term thrills typically deliver only short-term gratification. Even for serious, committed couples, sexual pleasure lasts only as long as the relationship does.

Though the virtues of patience and compassion relate to almost any area of life, chastity is specific to sexuality. Although chastity includes saving sex for marriage, it actually entails much more. You may be thinking, No way! That's too much to ask. Consider this example: if you were offered one hundred dollars today, would you take it? What if you were offered one hundred dollars today or one million dollars one year from today? Most of us, we hope, are wise enough to know that the one million dollars is the far greater deal, even though we must be patient.

When it comes to our sexuality, however, many of us are unaware or don't believe that there is "one million dollars" waiting for us. We've either seen or experienced the pain involved in broken marriages; or we don't believe we deserve such a powerful, sacrificial love; or we think we're simply incapable of loving on a deep level. We settle for the one-hundred-dollar experiences when one million dollars exists for each of us. We choose the immediate instead of holding out for the greater. Unlike the strictly future promise of one million dollars, chastity is not simply a future promise. It is more like receiving the money in daily thousand-dollar installments. Heather's choice not to have sex with Ryan was a difficult choice, especially during the romantic night in the park and knowing that many of their friends were sexually active. However, because they exercised the virtue of chastity, Heather and Ryan enjoyed a pure relationship where they did not use each other in any way. Their friendship continued long past the night in the park. They experienced a very romantic night and found alternative, unique ways to express their feelings for each other.

Choosing virtues over short-term thrills or what is popular requires faith. We must trust in something unknown—will the virtue really be worth it now or later on? Is God's plan for sex and relationships actually better? Whether we believe it or not, God really wants the best for each of us. Jesus said, *"Is there anyone among you who, if your child asks for a fish, will give a snake instead of a fish? Or if the child asks for an egg, will give a scorpion? If you then, who are evil, know how to give good gifts to your children, how much more will the heavenly Father give"* (Lk 11:11–13). God wants us to have relationships that are loving and satisfying. He doesn't want us to settle for mediocrity but to hold out for greatness, even if we must be different.

Spencer lived most of his young life as the popular "party animal" type of guy. When he began high school, he thought chastity was good, but he had his first sexual experience before he entered college. Most of his friends had "done it" by then, too. In college he was involved in a very serious and sexual relationship. Spencer was crazy about this girl, but the relationship slowly began to fall apart. They were no longer the friends they used to be, and he missed his relationship with God. One evening he told his girlfriend that he wanted to stop having sex—he hoped things could improve between the two of them. They decided to give it a try, but it didn't help. They broke up soon after because the relationship had become based on sex—not on their friendship. He experienced severe pain from losing the relationship. In his next sexual experience, he cared less and learned how cold and meaningless sex could be. This response scared him because he wanted sex to be special, to be something more.

He finally got sick of believing culture and his friends who claimed that being sexual was the best way to relate romantically before marriage. Even though sex felt great physically, there had to be something more for this twenty-five-year-old single guy. He then chose to trust in God's plan. Spencer made a new commitment to chastity and to wait until his wedding day to have sex again. This choice was very difficult and required him to grow in a variety of virtues. When asked about his decision and new lifestyle, he commented, "During this time of growing, I have never felt stronger in faith, joy, grace, and peace—I feel so alive!

In previous dating relationships, I always felt a need, like something was missing. I now realize God and his plan was missing. I finally understand how special it is to save sex in a relationship. I realize how much more incredible and awesome sex would be with someone you love, and so much more—sharing a spiritual love and a love in Christ that keeps going and growing—that is infinitely orgasmic. I won't settle for anything else."

God gave us the virtue of chastity so that we can experience greatness in all our relationships—not mediocrity, shallow love, or pain from the breakup of serious relationships. We are all capable of living this virtue but, in this day and age, chastity demands a different understanding of sexuality than the one promulgated by the culture around us. Like all the other virtues, chastity grows as we practice it. If we want the best in our relationships, we must live chastely—not because the Church or our parents say so—but because we want something different, something more, something better.

# CHASTITY

. . . . . . . . . . .

## What Does It Have to Do With Me?

Ask yourself the following questions (you can even raise your hand for a "yes" response if you wish or won't feel embarrassed): Do I want to be married someday? Do I want my spouse to be sexually faithful to me in our marriage? Do I want to experience deeply loving and passionate sex with my spouse? Congratulations! If you have answered "yes" to these three questions, you desire chastity. Now you may be saying to yourself, I didn't say *that*! However, if you desire faithfulness and passion in your marriage, then you desire chastity, at least in the future if not now.

A completely carefree attitude, or one with a lack of restrictions, toward sexuality in a culture would permit one to have sex with any person at any time for any reason. Since no good, humane culture tolerates rape—this is one of the basic elements of natural law[2]—the question for all of us is not whether we should have restrictions on our sexual activity but, rather, what restrictions should we have.

## What Chastity Is

Chastity is respect for our sexuality, so much so that sex is practiced in marriage only. For those who are single, this means respecting sex and waiting until marriage. For those who are married, this means respecting sex and having sexual relations only with one's spouse. For those who have made a religious vow or promise, it is giving themselves in service, sacrificing sex for God's kingdom. A good analogy is that sex is like fire—this metaphor is chosen not solely because

12

sexual passions can be ignited so quickly. A fire is great in the fire-place. It provides light and warmth and comfort; it's cozy and romantic. However, a fire on the living room carpet is dangerous; it can burn the entire house down. Likewise, sex outside of marriage can cause serious damage, whereas sex in the context of marriage is good for the relationship. Chastity respects the power and beauty of sex and desires never to misuse this incredible gift or cause harm.

## All of Us Want It Anyway

Few people who enter into a marriage want infidelity. Ironically, some people who are themselves unfaithful in their marriage desire their own spouses to remain faithful; yet affairs happen every day.

Consider this analogy. Imagine you are very sick and the doctors have diagnosed a swollen appendix that needs to be removed. Thirty minutes before your surgery, a guy with long hair and a dark tan, wearing a Hawaiian shirt and sandals, walks into your room. Though he's been out surfing for the last ten years, this very morning he decided that he really wanted to be a doctor. His desire to be a doctor is so strong that he wants to start today, with you. If this happened, would you let him remove your appendix? No! To be a doctor requires knowledge, training, and experience: things that don't happen simply because someone wants them or desires them.

Likewise, love is a habit and a virtue; it must be developed and practiced to be done well. Whatever virtues you practice during your dating is what you can expect in your marriage. Chastity prior to marriage goes a long way to ensure chastity within marriage.

## God's Design

Sex was discovered, not invented. It is more like Ben Franklin and electricity than Thomas Edison and the light bulb. God created sex and made it a good thing with a purpose and a function for everyone's benefit. Chastity recognizes this function and purpose to our sexuality.

Human sexuality has a twofold purpose. The first purpose is procreative, or life giving; sex brings new life into the world. The second purpose is unitive, or love giving, which brings the couple together, binding them closer. Both purposes are equally important; chastity recognizes that one is not to be included while the other is excluded; they go together. Sex is designed to reinforce the marriage vows. Outside of marriage, the meaning of sex is distorted or even undermined.

Another analogy for sex is that it is like a tool, such as a hammer or a screwdriver. Like any tool, it works best when it is used in the correct manner, and in the service of the purpose for which it was designed. If we use the screwdriver to pound a nail, we wreck the wood, perhaps the nail, and the tool itself. Using the wrong tool for the wrong purpose runs the risk of ruining the tool and the material. Sex was designed to perform a very specific function within marriage. It brings the couple together in an intimate way; it binds them to each other physically, mentally, emotionally, and spiritually; it reaffirms the vows that they stated on their wedding day. Since sex outside of marriage is being used for a purpose other than for which it was designed, it can harm both our sexuality and us.

## What Chastity Is Not

Chastity and abstinence are not the same. Abstinence is about what one cannot have or what one cannot do. For some, it means that as long as one isn't actually having intercourse, any other actions are acceptable. Others can practice abstinence without completely understanding the purpose for which their sexuality is designed. Chastity goes beyond simple abstinence. As speaker and author Jason Evert explains: "Chastity is what you can do and can have—right now: a lifestyle that brings freedom, respect, peace, and even romance—without regret."[3] Chastity is about what you can have now, beginning at the moment you make the decision for chastity. Chastity deals with our sexuality, not simply with acts of sex.

Similarly, chastity is not the same as virginity. There are some whose actions are unchaste but who do not engage in intercourse, thus retaining their virginity. There are some who have made poor decisions in the past, but who have chosen chastity and lived it faithfully afterwards. Chastity is not about one's past, it is about the present and the future. Not everyone can profess to be a virgin, but everyone can practice chastity. If you are no longer a virgin, you can experience healing and restoration; see the chapters on "Starting Over" (page 112) and "Trying to Undo the Past" (page 117).

## Chastity As Delayed Gratification

True love involves sacrifice. Few people like to hear that word. Too often we associate it with having to give up something good that we want. However, true sacrifice involves choosing a greater good at the expense of something less good, though perhaps truly good on its own. Often, we simply look at something as good or bad. If it's bad, we should avoid it; if it's good, then we should enjoy it freely. For example, there is nothing wrong with going out on a Friday night and having a good time with one's friends. However, if your grandparents are visiting from out of town, it is better and more loving to stay at home visiting with them and go out with your friends at a later date. It is the same as a savings account at a bank. Instead of spending the money immediately—and experiencing all the satisfaction that comes along with it—you can place it in an account so that it will be worth more later. When "later" arrives, your money will allow you to purchase more things or perhaps a more expensive item than you could have afforded earlier.

Chastity, as a part of true love, also involves sacrifice. It is giving up the good of sexual pleasure and the fulfillment of sexual desire until those emotions can be experienced within the context of marriage.

Chastity puts the good of true love in marriage over the immediate satisfaction of sexual desire. The delay today is an investment in something better in the future.

When you were younger, if you wanted something and your parents made you work for it, you probably valued it more. When we work for something, we treasure and cherish it more, it has more value for us, and we are more likely to take care of it. Who doesn't want to be valued and treasured and cherished? Guys, we know that cherish is a feminine-sounding word, but many married men will admit, at least privately, that they would enjoy being cherished by their wives. Living a life of chastity and accepting the sacrifices that accompany such a decision communicate clearly to your spouse that you valued him or cherished her long before the two of you married.

Chastity is about living real love, not accepting a cheap substitute. But it goes beyond delaying gratification; it also brings its own rewards and fulfillment.

## Chastity Is Its Own Reward

Some people are intrigued by chastity because it can lead to sexual satisfaction in marriage. This idea is a great one if God is calling you to the vocation of marriage. But some people are single, and others are called to the priesthood or the religious life. Chastity is just as valuable to them. Chastity means living out our sexuality as God intended it to be used: teen or adult; married, religious, or single. It is a virtue—a quality or characteristic of holiness to which we are all called. Chastity helps us to experience all relationships—friendship and otherwise—in the most loving way possible.

Chastity views our sexuality as a gift, something to be given completely and selflessly to another. Chastity can help us to become a pure gift to others, whether or not they become our spouse, by training us to love above all else.

Chastity transforms us into a pure gift by properly ordering the desires of our hearts. As the *Catechism of the Catholic Church* states clearly, either we are in control of our passions, or our passions are in control of us.[4] When sexual desire rules the heart, then love becomes directed by desire. This sequence is not in the proper order. In contrast, when we practice chastity, sexual desire becomes properly controlled by love. Love becomes the first and foremost desire in our hearts. Chastity doesn't destroy sexual desire, rather it puts it in its proper place, subject to love.

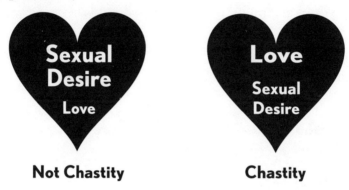

This proper order benefits everyone, whether or not he or she marries in the future. In the heart formed by chastity, outside of marriage, we know how to love others well and not focus on fulfilling our desires. When sex occurs in marriage, it is coupled with an outpouring of love, not simply to satisfy powerful desire. Sexual desires are under control so that one's spouse is never used but is always treated with love. In marriage, this properly ordered pattern of first love, then sexual desire, makes the difference between selfish sex and selfless—what we call great or chaste—sex. The passion of sex is intensified when love is foremost. Without chastity, there is always the possibility of sex without love, even in marriage.

## Chastity Purifies Us

Original sin has affected our sexual desires. Our fallen nature is such that we often tend toward the improper ordering of our desires.[5] In addition, our minds are exposed to a lot of junk, especially in our sex-saturated culture where so many views of sexuality are different from God's view. It's easy for us to be influenced by these cultural messages. The practice of chastity is a purifier for our sexuality; it helps us to keep our desires in proper order.

If we are very thirsty and come to a river, we may be tempted to drink right out of the river. Despite how clean it may look, however, we can never be sure that the water is safe until we have purified it. It is easier to drink it straight from the river, but it is better to wait until we have purified it. So it is with our sexuality; we might not want to wait to satisfy our sexual desires, but living chastely purifies our hearts so that our sexuality enriches us.

## Chastity Leads to Real Love and True Freedom

Chastity recognizes that we are all sexual beings. This part of our nature seems to be the strongest or most dominant element, especially when we are young. Whether or not we are currently sexually active in a relationship or are practicing chastity doesn't matter; we are sexual beings. The issue for every culture and every person in each culture is not whether to be sexual but rather how we will express our sexuality. In the next four chapters, we will spell out more clearly how chastity provides a framework for expressing our sexuality that helps us to experience real love and true freedom.

# Discovering the Unavoidable Consequences of Sex

## What Could Really Go Wrong?

Sure, we all know that sex is a physical act (duh!). Many teens therefore believe that if they avoid all physical consequences, such as STDs or pregnancy, sex is harmless. Not much else could possibly go wrong. However, millions of real-life stories, and even movies at times, prove otherwise.

Some movies that appear to show us nothing about chastity or truth surprisingly reveal glimpses of reality. Before Frau and Dr. Evil have sex in the movie *Austin Powers II: The Spy Who Shagged Me*, they make a verbal contract that things won't get "weird" because of having sex. In their vocabulary, "weird" refers to any of the emotional attachments that often come with sex. A day or two later, however, they both admit, "It got weird!" They couldn't keep their agreement. They wanted the sex to be only harmless fun, but it wasn't. Frau eventually becomes angry because Dr. Evil didn't telephone and asserts that she will never love men again. The "other stuff" is always involved, even when we try to pretend that it doesn't exist.

Whether or not we like it, sex creates more than just a bond between two bodies. Two hearts, two minds, and two souls are involved. The nonphysical aspects of sex may appear to be unaffected by sexual activity, but they are. In the chapter on "Great Sex" (page 40), we'll see how chaste sex in marriage blesses, improves, and increases the emotional, mental, and spiritual bond of a couple. Here, however, we will discuss how sex outside of marriage actually damages the heart, mind, and soul.

Sexual stimulation always affects the heart—for men and for women. This emotional connection is not a random occurrence but is inherent in the physical act itself.

> Women experience a flood of oxytocin—the same hormone that they produce in labor and in nursing a baby. Oxytocin causes a woman to be forgetful, decreases her ability to think rationally—and causes an incredibly strong emotional attachment to form with the man she is with. Men also produce some oxytocin during sexual intercourse. But their bodies also produce a hormone called vasopressin. Vasopressin, called "the monogamy molecule," kicks in after sexual activity, and its impact is to heighten a man's sense of responsibility.[6]

Biologically, God gave us hormones to make sure that sex touches us emotionally.

Sex is meant to produce such a strong bond that it helps keep husband and wife together for life. However, when the sexual bond is made prematurely—in relationships before marriage—problems arise. The physical bonding that comes from sex is inconsistent with a relationship that has not formed the emotional, mental, and spiritual bond of marriage. Some of the emotional consequences can be seen immediately; others are less obvious and may occur gradually, perhaps over a period of years.

"In college, I, Heather, was still deciding about chastity. While listening to sexually active friends and peers, I noticed the unexpected consequences of premarital sex—consequences far from the physical fun or love that my peers had expected. After college, I continued to observe in the circumstances of adult life all of the following consequences of sexual activity outside of marriage."

## Consequences of Sex Outside of Marriage

### 1. Devalued Sex

Every time we have sex outside of marriage, we are telling ourselves that sex is not *that* important to keep in marriage. We choose to give it less value than it is worth, even if we are in a relationship in which we really love each other. We reduce sex from a permanent gift to a temporary loan.

### 2. Stuck in Unhealthy Relationships

Most people find it difficult to leave the security and attention of a romantic relationship. When the sexual bond is added to the mix, the difficulty is compounded. Many relationships last longer than they should because of this bond.

### 3. Poor Communication and Problem-Solving Skills

A couple not living chastely often allows the physical acts to dominate the relationship at the expense of intellectual, emotional, and spiritual growth. Sexually active couples often turn to sex to resolve problems. Frequently, their relational time is spent making out or having sex rather than making conversation. While the physical aspect of the relationship may develop, other aspects suffer.

> Mike says, "I wondered if Deena wasn't the one for me. After we fought, however, we typically ended up having sex, and then when things returned to normal I didn't worry about our relationship anymore. Everything seemed fine and Deena was wonderful as long as the sexual relationship existed. Once we stopped having sex, however, and tried to solve issues simply through communication—wow, I realized she really wasn't the right person for me."

## 4. Stunting of Personal Growth

Young couples can get so absorbed in a sexual relationship that they isolate themselves from other activities, hobbies, and relationships that can help them grow as a person.

## 5. Feelings of Jealousy and Suspicion

The bond that sex forms is designed to unite husband and wife completely. In marriage, great security flows from this union. Outside of marriage, this false sense of union creates tremendous insecurity. Women tend to become "clingy" and guys may become more possessive.

## 6. Feeling Used, Experiencing Lower Self-Esteem

In a sexual relationship, sex is often the top priority. This usually leads to one and sometimes both persons feeling used.

> Jessica, a young adult, says, "It certainly didn't boost my self-esteem to know he drove two hours to meet me just because he wanted to make out. When I realized he didn't want to talk or just hang out, I knew he was using me for the make-out sessions. Although he claimed otherwise, his actions proved that he didn't care about my heart at all."

## 7. Worry About STDs or Pregnancy

> Missy saved sex until college. There she met someone she thought was the most incredible guy. She wanted her first time to be special and really thought it would be with Carl. However, in her first sexual experience, with a condom for protection, she contracted a STD. At the age of twenty-eight, all of her reproductive organs were removed because of the effects of the disease. Missy will never be able to have children.

A condom can't protect against everything, and many STDs are contracted from skin-to-skin contact, such as HPV (human papillomavirus). HPV alone is found in 75 percent of all sexually active Americans. This disease is rarely detected (for example, there is a visible symptom in only 8 percent of men who are infected), yet HPV causes 99 percent of all cervical cancer in women.[7] If you're sexually active and not worried about STDs, you should be. Just this one STD could easily and invisibly creep in and kill or sterilize you or the one you love.

## 8. Lack of Trust or Fear of Future Commitments

When relationships break apart, pain often follows. When we are hurt, our natural inclination is to protect ourselves. When we are hurt emotionally from sex, our protection is frequently to trust less and not to give our hearts completely to someone again.

## 9. Feelings of Depression and Suicide

Occasionally, the pain of breaking up is too much for a person to bear. Studies prove that significantly more sexually active teens are depressed and attempt suicide than teens who are not having sex.[8]

> Brian and Eileen were madly in love with each other during high school. They had sex and experienced the bond that results. When she broke up with him at the end of their senior year, he fell into a severe depression and ultimately committed suicide. The pain of losing Eileen was too intense for him to bear.

## 10. Feelings of Guilt, Shame, or Regret

When we have premarital sex, we can experience guilt, an appropriate sense that we've done something wrong. We can experience shame, feeling that we are unworthy because of what we have done. We can be embarrassed by what others might think of us. We can experience regret, realizing that we hurt others or ourselves through what we've done.

## 11. Blurred Perspective of One's Partner

We can develop a skewed view of our boyfriend or girlfriend. Once the sexual bond is formed, we become attached to the other person and begin to think more highly of him or her. In marriage, this outcome is very healthy; the sexual bond helps keep the relationship strong and united. Outside of marriage, this bond can be very unhealthy.

After just kissing Chad, I, Heather, ignored my friends who informed me of his lack of faith and his involvement in drugs. I was in such awe of his charm and good looks that I didn't care so much about other things. Wrapped up in kissing, I almost overlooked some major lifestyle differences. If we had had sex or had progressed further physically, I might have stayed with Chad.

## 12. Reduced Sexual Anticipation for Marriage

Sexual discovery for a couple can be such an adventure. Yet if a couple consummates their union before marriage, how much is there to anticipate on the wedding night, honeymoon, and during the early years of their marriage? Some resorts claim that more and more honeymoon couples seek outdoor activities; the bedroom is no longer the most appealing part of the honeymoon.[9]

## 13. Comparisons to Past Lovers

The sexual memory is strong. We remember moments of great vulnerability and intimacy much more than other activities. Practically speaking, we also remember what arouses someone and bring those memories and experiences with us into the marriage bed. An experienced spouse can make comparisons. An inexperienced spouse could struggle with ghosts of an experienced spouse's former partners.

Jennifer admits, "I know that my husband had been with others before me. Sometimes I catch myself wondering if I am as good as they were, if he hopes I'd be better, and if what we share is possibly a letdown to him after all he's experienced. Ideally, the mere physical stuff of the past shouldn't matter. I know he loves me more than them, but I also realize that he shared his soul and heart with these women as well. As much as I had hoped that his past wouldn't matter, these thoughts do cross my mind."

## 14. Distance From God

Sexual sins are serious because they are a misuse of a gift God has given us. Imagine that you spent hours putting together the perfect Christmas present for your mom. Now imagine that as soon as she opened it she said, "This isn't what I wanted," destroyed it, and threw it into the trash. You'd probably be more than a little hurt by her reaction, and it would no doubt have an effect on your relationship with her. This is similar to our relationship with God and how we often treat his gift to us of sexuality. For those who have had pre-marital (fornication) or extramarital (adultery) sex, Saint Paul writes: *"Fornicators, idolaters, adulterers…none of these will inherit the king-dom of God"* (1 Cor 6:9–10). It is our choice, not God's, to walk away from the graces he gives and our relationship with him. He desires that we live in real love, that we always respect the power and gift of our sexuality, and experience nothing less than its highest expression.

Obviously, not all of these consequences will happen every time sex is undertaken outside of marriage. Some repercussions occur every time, such as distancing ourselves from God and the devaluing of sex. Some may never affect a sexually active individual, such as feelings of shame or depression. Of course, these negative consequences can take place in nonsexual relationships, but they are less likely to occur and are typically less intense. Many teens think the negative consequences of living unchastely won't happen to them. Some teens think they are mature enough and ready to handle the consequences. In reality, however, neither thought can stop the consequences of sex outside of marriage.

> Hunter writes: Because I am an adult, twenty-two years old, and I waited until that age to make love, I thought that I was ready for the experience. What I did not realize is that it is not age that makes one ready for such a thing, but a full commitment in marriage that must be present first. I do regret my decision because I found that sexuality is empty without a higher level of committed internal feelings.

We could fill this book with story after story of people we know who have experienced many of the negative consequences of sex outside of marriage, but this is not our focus. Mentioning these stories here lets you know these consequences truly exist, that God believes we deserve better, and, more importantly, that sex should always be connected with real love, as described in the next chapter.

# EXPERIENCING
# REAL LOVE

· · · · · · · · · · · ·

## Isn't Sex the Natural Expression of Love?

Do you want to be a great lover? Who doesn't want that? To be great at loving friends, family members, and even in the bedroom, we must first understand love and then practice it as frequently as possible. To understand love, we must look past the media myths that love is what simply feels good at the moment. Contrary to music-video messages, great lovers aren't the men or women who can bring the sexiest partners to bed. In reality, being a great lover is much different: it requires that one actually loves others.

## Chocolate Love

We say we "love" so much in life, but do we actually love everything that we say we do? Consider this analogy: Jane loves her dad, and she loves chocolate. She often has good feelings about chocolate—a bar of pure European chocolate tastes so good when she has a sweet craving. Similarly, she often has good feelings about her dad, and she knows she loves him. So, does that mean Jane loves chocolate?

If chocolate disappeared, Jane wouldn't lose much sleep over it. She'd think, "What a loss! But I'll take vanilla pudding as a replacement." Jane certainly wouldn't sacrifice anything to help some chocolate that might be melting and stranded on the side of the street. That's because she uses chocolate—which is perfectly fine to do with food. Jane says she loves chocolate because it makes her feel good,

27

but she doesn't really love it. She uses it, and enjoys it, as much as possible.

Unlike chocolate, however, if something bad happened to her dad, she'd do anything for him. Jane wouldn't just think, "What a shame; dad is really ill. How I wish things were better for him! But there's always Mr. Ryan up the street." No, Jane might sell her car, even quit her job if necessary, to help him because she wants what is best for him. That is love. Good feelings are a bonus.

## Real Love

As Christians, we believe that God is love and that the model for real love is Christ. Talk about incredible love, God wants to be with us so badly that he died and suffered so we could be free from sin, live eternally, and constantly experience his love. If we consider Christ's dying on the cross for us as the ultimate sign of love, then real love doesn't require good feelings. Jesus sweated blood because he was so deeply anxious. He was betrayed by some of his closest friends and beaten by soldiers. That certainly didn't feel very good! Real love is not about feelings.

Real love is a decision and an action to do what is truly best for another. Often what is best for someone else is not what we ourselves want to do. Doing it anyway is love. Love is your tired friend staying up late to listen to you because you've had a bad day. Love is ending a date early to pick up your sister because she needs a ride. Love is sitting with your grandpa, even though he can't talk or respond. Love is being accepted and hugged after you've acted immaturely.

A good lover seeks to practice real love in all of his or her relationships. Just as Christ showed love for all people, so are we to love everyone.[10] Although your girlfriend and your mom, and your boyfriend and your dad, are all deserving of true love, there are different types of loving relationships.

## Love and Romantic Relationships

The strong, good feelings we have toward a member of the complementary sex are romantic feelings. Just as good feelings are not the same as love, romantic feelings and attraction are not the same as romantic love. Romantic relationships are defined by romantic feelings. However, it is unhealthy to build a relationship solely on romantic feelings. For example, Ed really has strong feelings for Ann. He likes being with her and hanging out with her. He also likes to put her down when he is upset. Since Ed's feelings are very strong, he really is "in love" with Ann. However, his actions are not very loving. Romantic love combines being in love with loving actions and attitudes.

## Love, Romantic Relationships, and Sex

Romantic love, of course, leads us to the thought of sex, which is only natural, since romance leads to marriage, which leads to sex. Sex is the fullest expression of romantic love that has been realized in a marriage. (Note that we didn't say that sex is the fullest expression of romantic feelings.)

As the previous heading suggests, sex should always be an expression of love. We should experience NOTHING EXCEPT LOVE every time we are involved in a sexual act. Unfortunately, outside of marriage, sexual acts fail to express love. We might want sex to express love, but for an act to say "I love you" it must be a loving act. Would it be truthful to tell your boyfriend that you love him while you take off his seat belt and drive faster, recklessly weaving in and out of traffic on cliff-side roadways? When we truly love others, we don't put their lives at risk. Similarly, no matter how much we might want sex to express love, outside of marriage it is not a loving act.

Paula and Jake believed they were in love. They had been friends
for years before they began dating, and being together made
sense. Paula cared very deeply for Jake, and the relationship was
serious. She gave all of herself to him, including her sexuality. As
grown adults, they were aware of all the possible consequences,
but they couldn't resist the desire to express themselves sexually. When they broke up, Jake was upset, but Paula was devastated. Jake moved on to another girlfriend soon after the breakup,
but Paula did not move on. For more than a year she cried on a
regular basis and felt as though Jake had walked away with a
major part of her.

Was sex a loving act for Jake and Paula? Was it a way Jake showed
his concern for Paula, his hope to protect her from harm? Was having sex a good way for Paula to protect Jake from guilt and comparisons in future relationships? Think back to the last chapter which
lists all the negative consequences that follows sex outside of marriage. Would I really love my boyfriend if I put him at risk for experiencing the damage that comes with premarital sex? No. It is not
loving to say to a girlfriend, "I love you so much that you might
become a teenage mother." It is not loving to say to a boyfriend,
"You might become depressed if we break up, or you might remember me when you're trying to have meaningful sex with your future
wife." And even if someone willingly allows you to put him or her at
risk, you're still not loving to do so. Pushing someone into ongoing
traffic, even if they ask you to do it, never qualifies as a loving act. It
is not loving to put anyone at risk, especially when such severe emotional, spiritual, and sexual injury comes with sex outside of marriage.

Some behaviors, such as riding in a car without a seat belt, have
the potential for harm. Sex outside of marriage, however, always
harms. At the least, it devalues sex and distances us from God. Love

begins when we choose a difficult path because it is best for the ones we care about. Chastity trains us in true love because it seeks what is truly best for others and ourselves. If you want to express romantic love, try a picnic dinner, long walks, gazing into each other's eyes, buying small gifts for each other. The number of romantic things you can do instead of sex is endless (for many more ideas, see Appendix B, page 167). Bottom line: real romantic love is to choose what is both loving and romantic.

Paula didn't date for years after breaking up with Jake. Finally, she met Tim. They hit it off and became serious rather quickly. As in her previous relationships, Paula thought sex was an expression of love, and so she and Tim began relating sexually. Paula didn't object to sex; she wanted that close bond. However, Tim began to notice that Paula wasn't quite herself. He sensed that the relationship could take a better path and decided to stop having sex with Paula. Tim didn't want Paula to be harmed in any way, even if they both enjoyed the sex. If they broke up, he didn't want to provide the type of hurt that Jake had. Although their relationship was good, its sexual nature was unloving. Because they chose to stop, their relationship improved and they were engaged many months later. Tim actually *loved* Paula—and still does. They learned and practiced real love. Choosing chastity deepened their relationship and led this couple to marriage.

## Experiencing Real Love

Loving others as Christ did is tough. It requires work. In our families, with people at school, and with strangers, we need to practice real love as much as possible if we want to be good lovers. We can sit at lunch with "the loner"—not because we want to, but because it might help the other person. We can take a younger sibling or cousin to a movie or baseball game. We might also ask our parents how they are doing—and then listen. If we practice love in unexpected or tough situations, we'll be pros when we fall in love with the right person. If we are called to religious life, we will be the most loving priest, sister, or brother we can possibly be.

The experience of real love is invaluable. However challenging, it is always worth it. If this sounds too difficult or even impossible, know that help is available. God does not demand more of us than his grace provides. Few guarantees exist in life, but here is one: If we strive to be in a good, close relationship with God, through his Son Jesus Christ—the best lover of all time—we will be the most loving people we can possibly be. Nothing can substitute for real love.

# FREEDOM
· · · · · · · · · · · ·

## Nobody Is Going to Tell Me What to Do

Most teenagers desire freedom from parental restrictions, Church guidelines, school rules, and even a book like this that might seem to tell them what to do. Authority figures, sometimes even friends, might come across as giving orders. Even though we may seem surrounded by rules and restrictions on all sides, other people cannot make decisions for us.

We *can* do whatever we'd like, whenever we'd like to do it. We are free. Yet, although we are free to choose behaviors, we are not free from the consequences of those behaviors. We are free to stick our fingers into a flame if we so desire, even if other people tell us we shouldn't. We are not free, though, from the blisters and pain that would result.

*"Then Jesus said…, 'If you continue in my word, you are truly my disciples; and you will know the truth, and the truth will set you free….Everyone who commits sin is a slave to sin'"* (Jn 8:31–32, 34). Throughout Scripture, God gives us his Word, which often contains guidelines and teachings, to help us make wise choices. God also gives us free will; we were not created to be God's puppets. If we choose to follow God's commands, then good consequences will naturally follow. Since God is love, everything he calls us to do is the most loving thing. His guidelines can be challenging at times, but they are always loving.

We can just as easily choose to use our free will to sin, to not follow God's Word. Natural consequences will follow such actions as well—and these repercussions may not be what we hope or expect.

The consequences of sin can, and often do, enslave us. We, the authors, know no one who would willingly choose to be a slave. And yet, when we use our free will to make poor choices, we are usually left with consequences, big or small, that enslave us instead of setting us free.

Dave, like most college freshmen, was free to go to parties and have a couple of drinks. He was also free to drive home after a few drinks. At one party, he wasn't legally intoxicated; he just had a buzz going. He was the most sober of his close friends, so it made sense that he would drive. But things in the car got distracting, and he accidentally hit a tree. He and the guy in the back seat behind him got out of the car with only scratches. His girlfriend in the front seat, however, has undergone numerous surgeries on her face from the accident. The young lady in the back seat died that night. Dave lost his freedom because he was in jail for months. Even worse, Dave says, is closing his eyes at night and reliving the scene of his friend's death—watching her drown in her own blood. The consequences of his actions failed to bring him freedom.

Is freedom, then, the ability to do whatever one wants whenever one wants to do it? If so, Dave would be free, but he is not. Freedom goes much deeper than just doing what we please. Freedom is an internal disposition. "Freedom is the ability to live responsibly the truth of our relationship with God and with one another."[1] Freedom is living and loving fully without enslavement to negative consequences.

God gives us the gift of our sexuality, and we are free to do whatever we want with that gift. We can choose to use it lovingly or to use it without concern for the consequences. Choosing to have sex outside of marriage might seem like a "freeing" thing—after all, our culture calls it sexual liberation. However, consequences follow our decision to use our freedom in this way, and those consequences enslave (as described in the chapter "Discovering the Unavoidable Consequences of Sex," page 19).

On the other hand, if we choose chastity, a wise and healthy choice, we experience the freedom Jesus was referring to: loving and healthy consequences. Chastity actually provides freedom on two levels: freedom from the many negative consequences associated with premarital sex, and freedom to live an exciting, healthy, romantic life in a variety of ways.

## Chastity Provides

### 1. Freedom to Experience Deep, Passionate Sex in Marriage

Chastity trains us to give sex the full value it deserves. The more we grow in the virtue of chastity, regardless of our past, the more we discover the fullness of sex as a lifetime commitment that says "I will be with you and love you for eternity." Chastity allows us to know nothing but the best of sex—as a total gift of self, full of deep passion and true love.

> Joshua writes, "On our honeymoon, Shannon and I didn't need a schedule packed with activities. We rarely left our hotel room! We had stored up passion; we were full of anticipation and pure desire. Everything was new, fresh, and intoxicating."[12]

### 2. Freedom to Date Creatively

Chastity shifts the focus of a relationship from "I want to get her alone" to "I want to plan a fun evening that she'll truly enjoy." It shifts from "how to turn him on" to "how to make him smile or laugh." When we really care about making the other person happy, we can find so many unique ways to spend time together without being sexual (see Appendix B, page 165, for ideas).

### 3. Freedom to Dump Losers[13]

When we are living chastely, we have the freedom to let go of poor relationships without an immense bond being torn apart.

"After about five dates with Adam, I, Heather, noticed some major personality conflicts. He really started to annoy me. Although the attraction was certainly strong enough early on, our choice to be chaste made it much easier for me to walk away from Adam. There weren't terribly hard feelings, and we actually remained friends."

### 4. Freedom to Trust and Be Trusted

In a world where infidelity seems too common, how will we know if our spouse will be faithful to us? How will we know we can last for decades with one person? Chastity teaches us to control our sexual desires before marriage so that we will be a professional at it when we are married.

### 5. Freedom to Know We Are Valued As a Person, Not Just a Body

When choosing chastity, we never need to wonder, "Is she with me just because she wants to be comforted or to feel sexy tonight?" "Does he laugh at my jokes just because he wants physical pleasure later on?" With chastity, we can be confident that the people we are dating are attracted to who we are as a person, not just to our body.

### 6. Freedom From STDs, Unplanned Pregnancy, and Worries Associated With Both

People who are practicing chastity have a zero percent risk of pregnancy or contracting an STD. Enough said.

## 7. Freedom to Develop Solid Communication Skills

Chaste couples do not rely on making out or having sex to resolve conflicts. Instead, they must find other—healthier—ways to resolve differences. Getting to know others' personalities, temperaments, and interests increases our ability to love them. Chastity helps us to develop a skill that is invaluable for friendships and romantic relationships.

> For six years Kelley and Jim saved sex for their wedding night. Kelley says, "We had fun going out and all, but mostly we spent our time talking. I knew Jim extremely well by our wedding day, and those communication skills we developed continue to help us in our marriage."

## 8. Freedom to Experience Peace of Mind

Peace comes with freedom from worries, anxieties, or guilt. It is much easier to sleep at night when we know we are not putting others at risk for serious consequences. Chastity gives us total peace through the truth that we are living out our relationships in the most loving way possible.

## 9. Freedom to Share a Unique Bond With Our Spouse

While we're still young, it's cool to dream about the most important relationship we'll have on earth—our marriage relationship. We need to save something for this unique person. I, Heather, have traveled the world, but I desire to give this most intimate part of myself to the most incredible man I'll ever know. Living chastely allows us—you and me—to start a completely new adventure with our spouse and look forward to a very exciting honeymoon and marriage.

> Tyler saved sex for marriage. Into his fourth year of marriage he
> said, "There is something cool in having only one person in the
> world who knows what you look like when you're having sex."

## 10. Freedom to Heal From Past Sexual Relationships

Previous sexual relationships often make us feel used, betrayed, ashamed, shallow, or unworthy of real love. These feelings can keep us from freely loving others and from experiencing love in return. We can, however, experience healing through many forms of God's love while living chastely.

Sacraments, Scripture, spiritual friends, and chaste romantic relationships open the pathway of Christ's healing power in our lives. (This process is described in detail in the chapter on "Trying to Undo the Past, page 117.)

## 11. Freedom to Be Intimate With God

Sin separates us from God. When we are choosing not to sin, we are free to be close to God. When we live chastely, we choose to stay in close relationship with the Creator of all love and pleasure.

## 12. Freedom to Really Love and Be Loved

Loving others is risky. Chastity removes the risk of suffering the negative consequences of loving others. We can be free to be vulnerable in love. We may be hurt or rejected, but not because we didn't love. Similarly, chastity commands true love from the people we date. We are free to demand a selfless love because we are able to love in this way.

To take freedom to a deeper level, consider this. Bob, a good friend of ours, once said that freedom as God intends is actually the ability to do whatever we want, whenever we want. At first, following the commands of Christ may seem restrictive and overbearing. However, the closer we get to Jesus, and the longer we are in relationship with him, the more we understand his heart. When our hearts are in tune with Christ's heart, we can do whatever we want. This is true because we will only desire to do loving things. Such freedom can't be reached perfectly until heaven; however we can certainly strive for, and get closer to, it on earth.

> Joanie writes: "When Chris and I started dating, we immediately moved into heavy make-out sessions and sexual arousal, although no intercourse. But during the years we were together, my interest in chastity grew. I worked on my relationship with God. During the last few months of our relationship, I didn't want to make out anymore. I didn't stop caring for Chris or make this decision to avoid guilt. I actually wanted to love him better. With my next boyfriend, a couple years later, neither of us even desired to make out. We were *very* attracted to each other and it wasn't easy, yet we lived chastely and knew heavy physical acts could ruin our friendship. I felt so free to love him as a person, not as a make-out partner, without fear of using him or of him using me."

Chastity is so much more than not having sex or avoiding bad consequences. Practicing the virtue opens us up to receive endless benefits—all the positive consequences and freedoms that naturally flow from following God's teachings. Most important of all the freedoms described in this chapter, chastity gives us the freedom to do what is ultimately most important for all of us—to love without bounds and to receive real love in return.

# GREAT SEX
· · · · · · · · · · ·

## But I Want Sex to Be Passionate and Exciting

Welcome everyone, especially those of you who have skipped straight to this chapter! Heather has graciously delegated this chapter to me, Pete, mainly because I'm the married one who has experienced this great sex we are encouraging. When asked if they want to experience great sex in their lives, almost all of the thousands of teens we have questioned have responded with an enthusiastic "YES!" Whether we are working with middle-school students or with juniors in high school, we find that everyone seems to desire great sex. To experience the deepest, most passionate sex, it is important to understand and live by five key sexual truths that are discussed in this chapter.

## Sex Is More Than a Physical Act

Almost every how-to manual and sexual guide focuses on the physical elements of sex. Just glance at the headlines of the magazines placed at the checkout counters of the supermarket: "Six Ways to Knock His Socks Off With a Kiss" or "How to Melt Him With These Sexy Moves." (These are not actual article titles copied from magazine covers, but they are close enough.) Guy magazines often tout such articles as "How to Perform and Have Her Begging for More," "Five Exercises to Boost Sexual Performance," or "Ten Dinner Menus to Increase Her Sexual Appetite." Our culture's unrelenting focus seems to be on the physical aspect of sex. The first key to great sex, however, is to recognize that sex goes beyond the physical.

We human beings have much more to us than simply our physical nature. We are complex beings, and the chart on this page emphasizes the four key components to our true identity. In addition to our body, we also have a mind, a heart, and a soul. Who we truly are becomes more and more clear as we move from one level to the other, going deeper into who we are. The first level, our physical nature, is the layer that everyone sees when they look at us. It is somewhat who we are, but none of us is limited or completely defined by our physical characteristics. The next level, our intellectual nature, includes our thoughts, how we think. Not everyone who sees us gets to this level. The third level, our emotional nature, usually takes more vulnerability to reveal. Often, it is only our close friends and family who experience us on this level. The fourth and deepest level is our spiritual nature, the complete and truest part of our being. Here dwell our deepest desires and motivations, our interior mistakes and triumphs, our sin and separation from God, as well as our moments of closest connection with the Divine. Many of us have a hard time revealing this side of ourselves to anyone, even to God, who, however, already knows us completely. To know anyone, even ourselves, well is to know the physical, mental, emotional, and spiritual sides of that person.

Our intellectual, emotional, and spiritual natures are fundamentally connected to our physical nature. That is, what we do with our bodies we also do with our minds, our hearts, and our souls. Shallow relationships and, therefore, shallow love exist primarily in the physical element. A deeper relationship, and therefore deeper love, involves a deep mental and emotional connection. The deepest relationships, and therefore the deepest love, are those in which our whole selves—physical, intellectual, emotional, and spiritual—are involved.

This description is based on our highest, most integrative human capabilities; it does not mean that there aren't people out there who are having great physical experiences through sex without practicing chastity. However, great sex, truly great sex, is more than simply the physical experience of a good orgasm and some good feelings. There is so much more to who we are—and to great sex—than simply the physical.

## Sex Is the Ultimate Physical Intimacy

Though some facts about the nature of physical intimacy are self-explanatory, I will offer a brief explanation. Intimacy, though often desired, is rarely defined. Simply put, it is the combination of closeness and familiarity that connects us with others. We have intimacy—closeness and familiarity—with our family members and our good friends. The biological reality of sex—two bodies being connected together—is the closest two people can be physically.

## Sex Does Not Equal Intimacy

I recently checked out some Web personals. Intimacy is one of the most frequently mentioned relationship goals. While guys admit a desire for intimacy, their ideas of intimacy probably differ from those of women. While sex is surely an expression of intimacy, many people who are looking for intimacy are looking for more than sex. Likewise, many people enjoy intimacy with people they are not sleeping with.

Intimacy can occur on each level of our being. Besides physical intimacy, we are capable of intellectual, emotional, and spiritual intimacy with others, with or without the physical intimacy of sex. We certainly would not forego some form of physical intimacy with those close to us, such as kissing our parents or hugging a friend, but we wouldn't have sex with all those close to us.

Intimacy goes beyond sex. Many people have sex and do not experience anything other than physical intimacy. Similarly, many people who experience intellectual, emotional, and even some physical intimacy are not engaging in sex. In a marriage, sex accounts for a small percentage of the time spent together as husband and wife. Even those who have sex frequently are nevertheless spending most of their married life together out of the bedroom; marriage is not an ongoing sexfest. A husband and wife must base their relationship—and their intimacy—on something more than the physical.

## Great Sex Involves Complete Intimacy

Great sex occurs when the ultimate physical intimacy of sex is combined with an equally close intellectual, emotional, and spiritual intimacy. Sex requires a complete physical vulnerability. Great sex also involves complete mental, emotional, and spiritual vulnerability.

In an earlier chart (page 41), we illustrated how the deepest relationships and the deepest love exist when we are connected on the deepest emotional and spiritual levels. This is also true for sex. The greatest sex involves vulnerability at the deepest emotional and spiritual levels. Sex that attempts to be vulnerable in one or more aspects of our humanity without being completely vulnerable in all aspects is less than what sex is designed to be.

Some people have a hard time seeing sex as a spiritual experience. What does God have to do with sex besides wanting us to save it for marriage? God desires to be a part of every aspect of our lives, including our sexuality. To be true to who we are, we must acknowledge that we are spiritual beings, and that we bring who we are spiritually to every experience we have. With sex we have the ability to stuff away and ignore our spiritual side, or to reveal and relish it in the act. Complete intimacy brings into the physical experience of sex a passion that encompasses all of who we are.

## Great Sex Involves Marriage

Marriage is a prerequisite for great sex. Only in marriage do we find the conditions necessary for the complete and total giving of oneself—physically, intellectually, emotionally, and spiritually—in the act of sex. What difference does marriage make? During a wedding, a man and a woman profess their love for each other and make a commitment before God and before the broader community to live out that love faithfully "until death do us part." This commitment is no small matter, though it may be treated as such by some.

The promises to love each other for better or for worse, for richer or for poorer, in sickness and in health, significantly alter a relationship. Up until the time of marriage, neither person is obliged to love the other unconditionally. If your boyfriend is arrested and goes to jail, you, the girlfriend, have the option and the freedom to dump him. If your girlfriend is in an accident and becomes a quadriplegic, you, the boyfriend, have the option and the freedom to stop dating her. If you are married and these things happen, you are to honor the "for worse" and "in sickness" parts of your marriage vows. If this sounds serious, it is. The marriage promises are a major commitment to love another—truly love another—forever.

The flip side of this commitment is that while you are professing love and commitment to her or him, she or he is professing the same to you. Nothing is more freeing to the human spirit than knowing that we are loved for who we are and that someone will never leave us. This love is a reflection of the unconditional love that God has for each of us at all times and without fail.

Similarly, a great freedom sexually comes from being accepted fully and unconditionally by another person. In this context, the security that results from being in a professed, committed, and deeply loving relationship allows us to give ourselves freely and completely, and we can experience the deepest levels of intimacy. This vulnerability in sex can only happen in marriage.

Outside of marriage, we cannot give ourselves completely to another person in sex. Physically, we can give most of ourselves but typically not our fertility. People who engage in premarital or extramarital sex rarely want to conceive. If we have not made a commitment to be together forever, we have not made a commitment to raising a child and a family together. Without that commitment, we are not free to give our full physical selves, which includes our fertility.

Likewise, because we have not made a commitment to love unconditionally, we cannot give ourselves to another without the fear of rejection. If we give our full minds or hearts to another, we cannot be assured that those will be treasured for the gift of self that they are. They may be used and then thrown back at us when the relationship is over.

Finally, outside of marriage we cannot give our full spiritual selves to each other. Sexual activity outside of marriage, by its sinful nature, separates us from God. Without God's graces and blessing, we must hide our soul and avoid spiritual truth and vulnerability.

Only in marriage, within the context of promised unconditional love, does the capacity and freedom for giving ourselves fully and completely exist. This is not to say that marriage magically creates these conditions. Regrettably, fear of rejection is present in some marriages. This situation is less than what any marriage should be and reflects more on the couple than on the value of marriage itself. The promises exchanged during the wedding ceremony are only as good as they are lived out in day-to-day marriage. The extent to which a married couple is able to live out their professed love is the extent to which they will be able to experience the conditions required for great sex.

Daryl was a popular jock in his high school. Sleeping around was part of his M.O. and was something he never thought twice about until he was in college. There he met Angela, whom he was really interested in dating; but she was not interested in dating him. She had made a faith-based decision to choose chastity. Daryl had turned his back on both faith and chastity, and Angela would only date him if he changed. This seemed strange to Daryl, but he began to explore both because of his interest in Angela. Eventually, Daryl made his own decision for chastity. Though his relationship with Angela didn't work out, Daryl stuck to his decision to be chaste. Even when he was engaged, he remained chaste. His first engagement did not end in marriage and, before he started dating his wife, so did two other serious relationships. For the six years that he lived chastely, Daryl grew in his understanding of the meaning of sex. On his wedding night, he and his wife enjoyed tremendous passion and romance. For him, the sex in his marriage is so far superior to the casual sex he experienced in high school—it isn't even worth trying to compare them.

## God's Design for Our Sexual Life Is Best

Let me be clear; this type of marital sex is not some out-of-reach ideal. This total commitment is what marriage and sex is designed to be. Many choose relationships that are less than what God desires for their lives. People who choose chastity are choosing to hold out for this type of great sex in their marriages.

# HAVING IT YOUR WAY

## Can't I Define the Meaning of Sex?

During high school, Justin and his first serious girlfriend chose to have sex. At the time, Justin believed sex was fine within serious relationships. By the time he reached his mid twenties, however, he had broken up with his first girlfriend and had experienced many relationships of varying length and depth. He eventually found himself in bed with just friends, even with women he would never choose to date. Then he met Rachel, the woman of his dreams. She had chosen to save sex for marriage. Sex meant so much to her; the value she put on the act was incredibly high. Justin realized that he conditioned sex to be merely a sport—just a physical activity he enjoyed with many people. During their engagement, Justin knew that the act he and Rachel would experience on their wedding night would mean something entirely different to each of them. For her, sex meant everything. For him, she was just the next and last woman.

The great sex described in the previous chapter sounds good. Many people desire great, meaningful sex in marriage and great sex before marriage, too. Can't you have both? No. No matter how we use sex, no matter what meaning we give it, outside of marriage sex is altered into something much less than a gift. The good news is that through the faithful practice of chastity, we can gain an appreciation for sex, no matter what we have done in the past.

## The Language of Sex

Most people in this world will be married. Most married people de-sire sex to be powerful, meaningful, and a sign of permanence in the marriage. Sex speaks a language, the language of giving ourselves to another person. John Paul II says that sex speaks "the language of self-donation. This is the language God built into it, and it is the language the heart hears....It is a language of permanent love and com-mitment, 'for better or worse.'"[14] Not only is this the ideal and best meaning of sex but also the true meaning of sex as it was created.

Like Justin, however, we have choices. We can allow sex to be a gift, a complete donation of self. Or we make it mean something else: "I give myself to you for a few months or years" or "I give myself to you for the night." In such cases, sex is not a gift, but instead merely a loan. A loan for a moment or even for several years is far different from a true gift, especially a gift that keeps on giving for a lifetime.

## Devaluing the Gift

When we loan ourselves out, it affects the gift. We tarnish the gift within us. Often the most profound but least visible damage that occurs from sex outside of marriage is what we will call the "dull-ing," or devaluing, of the gift of sex. Every sexual act outside of marriage reinforces the idea that sex is not important enough to save for marriage, decreasing the value of the gift. The dulling always occurs, one way or another.

## Dulling the Ability to Give Wholeheartedly

People who want sex before marriage to be meaningful often try to include their intellectual, emotional, and spiritual selves. When the sexual relationship ends, the pain of the breakup is intensified on the intellec-tual, emotional, and spiritual levels. This heartache, left untouched by God's healing, limits our future ability to give ourselves fully. As a result, the gift of sex has been dulled.

## Dulling As Protection

The second consequence of dulling results from trying to protect ourselves. Either from the experience of being hurt or from a desire to not be hurt, we can intentionally withdraw, repress and therefore dull the intellectual, the spiritual, and especially the emotional dimensions of ourselves in sex. This treats sex as only or mostly physical. This type of internal protective allows us to remain sexually active and seem emotionally healthy. Later, when we enter marriage and desire the complete giving of ourselves, we are incapable of doing so. Because we have trained ourselves to be sexual on a merely physical level, complete intimacy is rarely achieved. Sex in marriage will be less than what it could be because of dulling.

## Results of Repeated Dulling

Popular entertainment often epitomizes this extreme dulling as one person moves from one partner to another in seemingly perfect bliss. Avoiding emotional entanglements allows us to have sex or to make out without regret or pain in the morning. We might seem emotionally strong by not caring too much when a sexual relationship ends. However, a big difference exists between being emotionally healthy and emotionally absent.

Yet, we need not be entirely cold or unemotional sexually to dull or diminish sex. Seemingly normal, stable, healthy individuals do this when they move from one serious relationship to another. After several broken sexual bonds, we simply cannot offer all that we have given in the past. Although we might experience very good feelings for another in the sexual experience, it is not nearly as strong emotionally as it could be.

Dulling can be demonstrated by using an analogy that features duct tape. God has given us this powerful gift of sex to be a force binding us to our spouse. When we use that gift in other ways, it attaches us to another person, much like duct tape sticks to someone's arm. When the relationship breaks up, it feels like the duct tape being pulled off a person's arm. Removing the tape causes some pain to the arm and leaves some of the person, usually hair, on the tape. Because duct tape is strong, we can use the same piece again, this time on someone else's arm, much like we can give ourselves to someone else again. However, when that relationship breaks up and the duct tape is removed, it doesn't cause as much pain because only a little hair is removed. If repeatedly stuck on someone, what was once a powerful bonding force will no longer stick to anything. So it is with our sexuality. Engaging in premarital sex lessens the bonding ability of sex. When we finally need the bond, we are unable to create it.

Either through the pain of heartache or our attempts to avoid and numb pain, we damage the intellectual, emotional, and spiritual aspects of sex, altering and diminishing the gift, as visually represented in the diagram that follows.

# Physical
### ~~Intellectual~~
### ~~Emotional~~
### ~~Spiritual~~

Focusing primarily on the physical act is shallow sex. God wants us to experience the fullness of sex with all of its depth and beauty. The more we engage in shallow sex, the less we can function sexually on the intellectual, emotional, and spiritual levels. Therefore, we often believe merely great physical sex is the best that it gets.

Drew, like Justin, had sex before marriage. He would say, "Sex is just a thing between two consenting adults, not always meant for love. You can decide that it's not going to hurt your relationship—the emotional stuff doesn't need to get involved if you don't want it. Sex can be just a physical thing." This mentality—fueled by pornography and his relationships with women—followed him to marriage. As a Christian man of the community by the time he got married, it was common for other people to comment on how he seemed to have a very good marriage. However, other people didn't know what was happening in the bedroom. Sexually, the first few years of marriage were very difficult for Drew and his wife. Both were subconsciously bothered by memories of the past and images of how physical sex should be. Drew believed his wife should please him and couldn't understand her desire for emotional intimacy. He began to notice that the way he pursued his wife sexually was less than honorable. Even though he tried to please her, she felt used because the focus was always on physical arousal—not on deep intimacy. Because Drew loved his wife, he knew he needed to change. Although they never cheated on each other, they realized they weren't living chastely or experiencing the fullness of sex. Drew wanted sex to be intimate on all levels with his wife. But it took years of a commitment to chastity and a great deal of transformation to move past the physical mentality he had held for so long. He now admits that sex is much better and richer but wishes he had chosen chastity years earlier.

Many married couples experience the lack of deep intimacy that Drew and his wife endured. It often takes years, sometimes counseling, and lots of work for couples to heal the intellectual, emotional, and spiritual damage of dulling. To see sex only as a loving, complete gift of self takes years of practice and training. Chastity is that training. Chastity requires that we give sex the full meaning and value it deserves. If a couple enters marriage with a chaste perspective on sex, most likely they will not struggle with years of trying to undo shallow or painful experiences of the past.

Catherine was a popular girl in high school and enjoyed dating. During her first few years of college, she experienced several sexual relationships, including some of the heartache of break-ups. Then she dated Matt. They decided early in the relationship that sex would mean very little to them. They would keep the sex casual, without emotional entanglements. However, Catherine couldn't really follow through on that plan. She was starting to care for Matt and was therefore devastated when they moved apart (even though she kept silent about her feelings and always seemed strong). Around that time, she learned about chastity. She knew she was experiencing meaningless sex but also knew deep in her heart that she wanted real love. Dreams of marriage, security, and children were secret, but strong in the depths of her being. Once she realized the beauty of chastity, she knew it was the only route to experiencing what she most desired. She soon made a commitment to chastity and turned to God to receive healing from previous sexual relationships. Through those years of living chastity, she not only began to believe in the fullness of sexual intimacy, but she lived it by not harming the gift anymore. By her mid twenties, she married the man of her dreams. They lived chastity from the moment they met and experienced an incredible honeymoon to boot.

Whether we dull sex in small or big ways, we are trying to change the meaning of sex to something more convenient for us, but we only damage our sexuality. Unlike many other life experiences, sex wasn't created for a "live and learn" mentality. Sex is different. It was created to say to another person, "I give myself entirely to you for a lifetime." If we can't say that every time we have sex, we are "having it our way," and we're missing out on the beauty, meaning, and depth of our sexuality. However, the longer we live chastity, the easier it becomes to believe sex is a gift, not a loan. Practiced chastity makes self-donation and complete acceptance in married sex not only natural but also powerful.

# IF NOT SEX, WHAT CAN I DO?

## How Far Is Too Far?

When it comes to intimacy, the million-dollar question is "How far is too far?" Males and females are attracted to one another—it's a natural, healthy part of life to desire a relationship with members of the complementary sex. With intercourse out of the question, there are ways to grow in intimacy with another and yet remain chaste. Some people hold that everything up to a certain point is healthy and everything beyond that point is "too far." While there are some clear boundaries, every couple must evaluate for themselves what is holy and healthy in regard to their physical intimacy. If you hope to develop healthy physical relationships, read on.

## Affection Versus Lust

Since every physical act sends a message—even a punch speaks volumes—we must consider what our actions will "say" before we act. In romantic relationships, the goal is to communicate in a loving, giving manner—to be affectionate. Affection is defined as "tender and loving feelings" or a "stirring of loving emotions," and it stems from a desire to affect someone's heart, mind, or soul. Affection says to another, "I care for you so much that I've run out of words to say and want to show you" or "I want to give you a physical experience that touches and blesses you intellectually, emotionally, and spiritually." Affection is the outward expression of something that is occurring within the couple internally; this something is more than physical attraction.

On the other hand, lust is excessive sexual desire not controlled by concern for another. Lust does not give; it takes for itself. Lust is an appetite that seeks to satisfy itself at the expense of another and is unconcerned with intellectual, emotional, or spiritual health. It is never healthy, loving, or giving, even in marriage.

Obviously, affection should be the primary goal of every healthy couple—never to use each other for physical gratification, but rather to love each other. To ensure that physical acts are affectionate, a couple must thoughtfully decide when and how to progress physically in a healthy manner.

## When to Be Physical?

To know whether a relationship is ready for physical affection, one must first examine the intellectual, emotional, and spiritual bonding of the relationship, or the "friendship" elements. A healthy romantic relationship should be based on a friendship, with physical acts being the "icing on the cake." A cake isn't made with icing in the batter; it would never rise. You must first make the cake (relationship) with the essential ingredients of flour (great conversation), sugar (fun together), eggs (similar moral values, spiritual agreement), and brown sugar (respect, honor). When all of these work together and rise, add the icing (physical intimacy). A cake, like a romantic relationship, is incomplete without icing (at least some physical sign that this person is more than a friend). Although no time is specified for adding the icing, the intellectual, emotional, and spiritual intimacy should come first.

As a relationship deepens, the friendship elements should continue progressing at a steady rate, and the physical should slowly follow. In this way, the other intimacies support the physical. All healthy physical acts should be an outpouring of the strong personal connection of the couple. Acts of physical affection progress as the friendship and relationship grows, with the couple eventually arriving at a place where marriage makes sense physically, intellectually, emotionally, and spiritually.

## Elements of a Romantic Relationship

The physical connection is important because it distinguishes a romantic relationship from a friendship, but it shouldn't be the foundation or the first element of the relationship. The friendship aspects of the relationship may not grow exactly as sequenced in the graph, and that is normal. Some couples connect and grow spiritually before they do intellectually or emotionally. The sequence of growth for the friendship intimacies is not as important as the fact that they should develop before the physical.

## How to Be Physical?

Appropriate physical affection at each stage of a romantic relationship will be different for each couple. Most important is that each couple should move slowly physically and focus on affectionate acts only.

Many young people have the misconception that the only options in physical intimacy are kissing, touching, and then sex. Desmond Morris compiled a list of stages of marital intimacy. We've adapted it somewhat to illustrate the many physical ways to show someone you care. The first six stages are almost always, on their own, signs of affection. They are...

1. Eye to body (looking at someone in a different way than how you would look at a family member)
2. Eye to eye (connecting with intense eye contact)
3. Voice to voice (revealing different aspects of self by using a unique tone of voice)
4. Hand to hand
5. Arm around shoulder
6. Arm to waist

The next three stages can be affectionate, but they also have the potential to become lustful. Depending on the depth of the relationship and the couple's intentions in the act, they may or may not be healthy.

7. Face to face (kissing, from a cheek peck to open-mouth)
8. Hand to head (caressing the face and embracing the head during a hug or a kiss)
9. Hand to body (nonsexual discovery of his or her body)

The remaining stages are direct sexual stimulation and should be reserved for marriage.

10. Mouth to breast
11. Hand to genital
12. Mouth to genital
13. Genital to genital[15]

## Avoid Lust and Sexual Stimulation

As a relationship develops, conditions can be present in any of the stages that will lead to too much or inappropriate physical intimacy. If one hasn't bonded intellectually, emotionally, and spiritually with another, yet acts physically out of a desire to be physical, lust has control. Relationships fail to develop in a healthy manner when lust takes over. Lust focuses on the physical bonding at the expense of the other aspects of the relationship. Lust does not require intellectual, emotional, or spiritual bonding, so it does not need friendship to grow. For couples who focus primarily or too early on physical acts, the other three intimacies typically become stunted, take longer to develop, and are always overshadowed by the physical. A kiss or prolonged embrace becomes meaningless if the understanding of another's heart, mind, and soul is lacking.

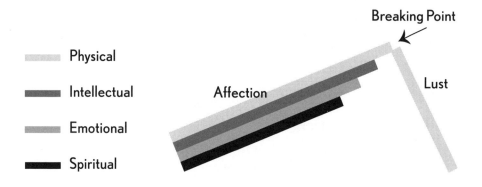

When the physical is not supported by a growing intellectual, emotional, and spiritual connection, the focus becomes lustful. We will call this the "breaking point." How far is "too far"? Everything after the breaking point—the switch from affection to lust—is too far, unhealthy, and therefore sinful because it is not supported by the other aspects of intimacy. How soon the breaking point is reached will differ from couple to couple. For those who have had previous sexual experiences, the breaking point can come much sooner than for others.

In addition to lust, purposeful sexual stimulation before marriage is "too far." Oral (mouth to genital) and manual (hand to genital) stimulation, cybersex (stimulation from pictures or words on a computer), phone sex (stimulation from conversation only), and dry sex (sexual gyration and possibly partial penetration with clothes on) can cause many of the same emotional consequences as intercourse.

Sexual stimulation before marriage is also unhealthy intellectually. Logically, it is obvious that purposeful stimulation is designed to lead to intercourse. It's deceptive to prepare someone for nothing. Even if a male's brain agrees that a certain point is "how far" he wants to go, his body is inclined to go further. It is repressive for couples to be turning each other on just to "shut down" before intercourse. God designed sexual stimulation to be brought to completion. Training ourselves to turn off the stimulation just when it's supposed to get good is dangerous. It decreases our ability to give freely in marriage. In regard to sexual acts, God even warns us, saying, *"Do not stir up or awaken love until it is ready!* (Song 8:4). Whatever leads an individual or couple to sexual stimulation should be avoided before marriage to avoid repression. (You can read more on the topic of repression in "Laying Aside a Myth," page 74.)

> Steven had experienced sex in the past, but desired to live chastely. From his previous relationships, he knew that "French" kissing aroused him and made him want to go further. When he started dating his now wife, they made the decision to not kiss in that way. French kissing was one of Steven's breaking points.

Steven's breaking point may be different from Heather's or Pete's, but it's important for every individual, and couple, to know and respect their own personal temptations to lust.

## What Can I Do? Focus on Affection!

A healthy couple will recognize their breaking point and avoid it. This knowledge surfaces either from the wisdom of others or from personal experience—individually or as a couple. If a couple moves slowly and keeps motives in check, they do not need to experience their breaking point to know where it exists. A healthy couple will show physical affection without putting each other on the brink of sin.

In a loving relationship, if one senses the breaking point soon approaching, he or she will stop the other so that together they can keep the relationship chaste.

> Lana and John decided to move slowly physically. During the rare instances in which they were alone and relating romantically, they chose to kiss the other's forehead if it appeared to either one that they could be heading towards lust or stimulation. This indicated that they needed to slow down physically. With the use of this easy and loving gesture, they chose to keep the focus on affection.

Fun, healthy dating avoids bringing each other to the breaking point or leading the relationship into lust. True chastity allows us to walk away from every date with the respect that we deserve. Dating someone who doesn't want to push you is freeing and fun!

These guidelines for healthy relationships might seem challenging; however, we must consider the perspective from which they emanate. When it comes to suggestions and rules from the Church, we often become frustrated and view them as obstacles or fences that keep us from experiencing the other side. We focus so much on "the fence" and what's on the other side that we miss what is around us. Instead of staring at the fence, why not turn around and focus on enjoying all the beauty, fun, and peace that can be experienced within the boundaries?

Chaste couples will cherish and enjoy true physical affection. They will focus the relationship on "How can I be romantic and creative to show I care for this person within the bounds of what is healthy?"

instead of "How far can I push physical affection before we sin?" A healthy, chaste couple will slow down and savor the journey of discovery and the passion that builds as the relationship develops.

Brad enjoyed sex in previous relationships. However, he described how hugs and holding hands became almost meaningless in such relationships. Then, years after he committed to chastity, he met Mindy. They were good friends for months and bonded deeply, especially on a spiritual level. One night, while walking out into the cold air, Brad pulled Mindy's arms around him. They walked that way for a short time. Brad later commented on how cool it was to experience that small moment of affection with Mindy. He realized that living the virtue of chastity gave a simple act depth and power. It was just the start of an exciting new adventure.

# Just My Thoughts

## Why Do They Matter?

One of the unique traits human beings possess that animals do not is that all freely made actions have two steps to them. The first is the conscious thought that we should act in a certain manner. The second is the actual acting in that manner. These steps may occur so close together that we might think they happen simultaneously. Usually, though, a delay almost always occurs between the thinking and the doing. This delay is helpful; it allows us to evaluate all of the thoughts that pop into our heads and determine which ones are good to act on and which ones are not. For example, many people have been so angry they felt like strangling someone. Those who acted on that thought are most likely in prison.

Our thoughts are powerful. Every thought we have is a suggestion for action. Some thoughts inspire us to be creative; some nudge us into helping others; some help us understand ourselves or others. A strong connection exists between our thoughts and our actions. For example, we might become angry with someone and then think that our lives would be easier if the other person weren't around. Most healthy people would dismiss such a thought and not act on it. Some people, however, may begin to think about how they would go about getting rid of that person and even begin to plan how they would avoid being caught. A few might actually put the plan into action. The danger, of course, is that once someone's thoughts get to a certain point, it is easier to act on those thoughts.

Chastity is first and foremost about what we do with our bodies, respecting sex by the way we act. But chastity is more than just about our bodies; it also involves our thoughts. How we act sexually stems from our thoughts and beliefs about sex and about members of the complementary sex. Our thoughts have a strong influence on how we act. Similarly, when it comes to our sexuality, our brains have the ability to evoke physical responses. This brain-body connection is more prevalent among men, but women's brains also can have a strong influence on actions.

Therefore, if we want all our actions to be respectful, we must think respectfully about sex, not as something used for our pleasure. Chastity calls us to purity of mind. This purity of mind can be likened to the way in which accomplished athletes use their thoughts to help them become successful. Most great athletes visualize what is going to happen before it happens. They think clearly and deliberately about what they need to do and how to do it. A strong correlation exists between how well they visualize their moves and how well they execute those moves. Our actions—behavior—can also be powerfully influenced by our thoughts.

While they were dating, Ted and Sandy made a decision to save intercourse for their wedding night. As a teen and young adult, Sandy had tried to have sexually pure thoughts. Ted, however, had filled his teen brain with idea that sex was a major conquest that he could achieve in marriage. Upon entering their honeymoon suite, Ted practically attacked Sandy, rushing through the act of intercourse. Ted's actions left Sandy in tears and feeling used. Ted's vision was that sex was to be kept in marriage, but in marriage sex became a free-for-all. His thoughts about sex led to his behavior—behavior that was harmful to his wife and damaging to their relationship.

Do not be confused. Chaste people DO have sexual thoughts. But they do not allow these thoughts to lead to unhealthy thoughts or actions.

Consider three important elements of purity of mind. First, purity of mind involves how we think about others. If chastity involves respecting sex to the point of keeping it within marriage, then we should only be thinking about sex with the person who is married to us. However, this decision is challenging because our culture is saturated with sexual images and with advertising that is aimed at getting us to think sexually in many situations. Chastity calls us to think of people as persons, not as objects, for our pleasure. When we view members of the complementary sex as sexual objects, we fall into the sin of lust. Living chastely means avoiding lust by keeping our thoughts about others pure and respectful.

Second, our purity of mind is affected by what we allow our minds to see. The saying here is—"garbage in, garbage out." If we fill our minds with pornographic images, R-rated movies, and television shows that portray sex as being only about physical pleasure, we will find it difficult to think respectfully about sex. It is said that our brains are able to store every image and everything that we see or experience (even from our time in the womb); we lose only our ability to retrieve these things, not the things in our brains themselves. Living chastely means being selective about how many sexual images and what type of ideas enter our minds.

Third, how we deal with sexual thoughts that pop into our heads is a part of purity of mind. The case of unexpected sexual thoughts is a bigger problem for some than it is for others, and usually men struggle with this more than women; but these random mental temptations are an issue for almost all of us at some time in our lives. Unsought thoughts are part of our human nature and are not something that we can control. A strong connection exists between what pops into our heads and what we allow ourselves to view, so in that sense we can limit sexual thoughts by limiting our exposure to sexual images. However, even then they cannot be completely avoided.

The danger from random sexual thoughts arises when we entertain them for a while, turning them into disrespectful or lustful thoughts. The former are beyond our control; the latter are not. Living chastely involves not giving in to the temptation to turn random thoughts into lustful thoughts. (For help on dealing with lustful thoughts, see the chapters on "Laying Aside a Myth," page 74, and "How Can Men Live Chastely," page 144.) Everyone who is practicing chastity must deal with sexual thoughts. For some, this is more challenging than others, especially for those who choose chastity after having had sexual experiences.

Two closing thoughts are especially important here. First, God is merciful with our sincere efforts to live chastely. Second, purity of mind is important because without it impure actions come much easier. If we want to live chastely, we must be able to think chastely.

# KILLING IT SLOWLY

## Can't We Just Use Contraception?

No one reasonably disagrees with the fact that having sex has consequences. This is positive when, in the context of marriage, sex helps to form a tight emotional bond. This is negative when, outside of marriage, sex becomes devalued. Usually, when people talk about the consequences of premarital sexual behavior, they are referring to pregnancy and STDs. Given the attraction and pleasure of sex, it is not surprising that people have developed ways to attempt to enjoy the act without suffering any of these negative physical consequences.

During the last forty to fifty years, the changes in available means of contraception—the deliberate attempt to prevent pregnancy as a result of sex—and the changes in sexual behavior have seemed to go hand in hand; as more effective means of contraception have been developed, people have felt freer to engage in premarital sex, thereby creating a greater market for contraception.[16] Over that same time period, the once unanimous Christian opposition to contraception has been whittled down to one voice: that of the Catholic Church.[17] Even within the Church there is often great opposition to this teaching. This chapter will be a tough one to read because it goes against much of what is accepted in our culture. This chapter will look at why the Church opposes contraception and how it is contrary to true chastity.

## The Myth of "Safe Sex"

Many adults, trying to do the best for teenagers, make two false assumptions. The first is that people, especially teenagers and young adults, are going to have sex. Second, if these teenagers and young adults are having sex, they should at least be "safe" about it. These statements sound reasonable, even compassionate and caring; but they are not. It is realistic to state that some teenagers are having sex. It may even be realistic to say that half of them are having sex. It is unrealistic, however, to say that they must have sex, almost as if to say they are incapable of not having sex. Instead, hundreds of thousands of teens have chosen chastity or abstinence and are waiting until they are married to have sex. Contrary to rumored belief, no one dies from not having sex.

It seems caring to want to protect teenagers from things that are dangerous. An adult notices that a young person is engaged in harmful behavior and wants to provide him or her some protection from that harm. However, two major problems present themselves with this approach, one philosophical and one practical. Philosophically, handing a condom to a teenager to prevent the negative (physical) consequences of sexual behavior is like buying a five-year-old a pair of fireproof gloves so he or she can play with matches safely. Usually, the accepted practice is to teach the five-year-old not to play with fire. The only reasonable approach to harmful behavior is to avoid the behavior that brings harm or to stop the behavior if it already exists, not encourage it with protection.

Amy's mom knew her teen was having sex, and although she wished Amy would stop, she didn't think discussing the problem would end the behavior. Therefore, Amy's mom arranged for her to take the birth-control pill. Amy, now an adult, believes that her mom's approval of her contraception use subconsciously

> allowed her to be free from guilt and actually increased her sexual
> promiscuity.

On the practical level, condoms are not as safe as many people have been led to believe. Condoms are frequently advertised as providing protection from unwanted pregnancy and STDs. Although condoms do provide more protection from these consequences than nothing, they hardly qualify as a safety measure. The numbers on STDs alone is staggering: Studies show that nearly two-thirds of STDs occur in those under twenty-five, and one-fourth of all new cases are teenagers.[18] Frequently reported failure rates for condom usage range from 5 percent to 15 percent, and that failure rate is usually based on the condom's ability to prevent pregnancy over just a one-year period.[19] While pregnancy can only occur during a small window of time each month, STDs can be transmitted at any time. Also, studies have indicated that women on the birth-control pill have an increased risk of breast cancer.[20] Since STDs can lead to infertility, cancer and even death, and condoms provide little protection, their use can hardly be called "safety."

## Chastity and Contraception

For those who wish to live chastely, contraception is not an option. This makes sense prior to marriage—where using contraception means having sex before marriage which contradicts chastity—but the use of contraception within marriage is a more difficult prohibition to understand, especially when many married couples are choosing to use contraception. There are four key reasons why contraception and chastity are incompatible.

First, contraception violates the procreative purpose of sex. A natural cause-and-effect relationship exists between sex and pregnancy. The biological, and obvious, purpose of the act is to conceive children, much like the intended result of exercise is fitness. Procreation is not the sole purpose of sex, but it is the natural result. Often, people want the act of sex without the natural result of sex. This desire is much like wanting all the heat that comes from burning wood but none of the expense of purchasing the wood or the inconvenience of stacking logs and cleaning the fireplace. Few would find it acceptable to separate the love-giving dimension (such as a husband forcing himself on his wife) in the same way that contraception separates the life-giving dimension. Chastity is about respecting our sexuality—all of it—and contraception violates the part of our sexuality that is procreative.

Second, contraception fails to unite a couple completely. The second purpose of sex is unitive; it has the power to bring a married couple into a complete union. In an act of sex using contraception, the unity is compromised because neither the husband nor the wife is being united fully to the other. The gift of self is an incomplete gift because the couple withholds the gift of fertility from each other. Contracepted marital sex says, "I give myself to you, but not fully, I'm keeping my fertility for myself."

Third, sex in marriage is meant to be a renewal of the marriage vows, bringing us back to the graces of the sacrament of marriage. Part of the marriage rite in the Catholic Church involves answering "yes" to the question, "Will you accept children lovingly from God?" Contracepted sex says "no" to that vow. As a vocation, marriage is meant to be life-giving—both to the couple and to others. Instead of recommitting themselves to the marriage vows, the contracepting couple denies those vows. Most of us would not think of violating the marriage vow to be faithful; however, all parts of the vows are equally important.

Fourth, God has given human beings great power in being co-creators of life. Contraception closes God out of the co-creative act. Instead of being open to the possibility of God blessing them with a child, the couple is closed to it. This is a spiritual rather than a physical decision. God calls us to trust in him, to be open to his plan for our lives and families. The decision to contracept is a decision not to trust him completely.

There are many couples using contraception who attest to no harmful side effects. However, the damage caused by contraception is difficult to detect while it is happening. The best analogy here is that of a frog, a cold-blooded animal. A frog placed in a pot of boiling water will immediately hop out; it knows that the boiling water is harmful. However, the same frog placed in a pot of lukewarm water will stay there. If that same lukewarm water is placed on the stove and the temperature increased to the boiling point, the frog, unaware that it is in danger, will stay there as steam curls around its nostrils. When the damage is gradual, we can fail to be aware it is even happening. Contraception slowly destroys the unity between husband and wife and their relationship with God.

## The Catholic Church and Natural Family Planning

Contraception is not the same as birth control. There is an essential difference. Birth control is the process of spacing births and deciding when to expand one's family. The Church even states that married couples have a moral obligation to determine the size and spacing of their families, though not without prayerful discernment.[21] Contraception, however, is an immoral means of birth control. Couples who do not wish to have another child do so by refraining from having sex when intercourse could lead to pregnancy. A significant scientific development in the last half century allows women to recognize signs produced by their bodies that indicate fertility. Almost every woman, with a little bit of training, can learn how to know when she is and is not fertile.[22] The three natural methods of determining periods of fertility are generally referred to as NFP (Natural Family Planning).

Some people argue that there is no difference between NFP and contraception. Unfortunately, some people using NFP have a contraceptive mentality, such as "Pregnancy is a disease I need to avoid."

This mentality is in opposition to chastity, even if their means is not. Contrary to popular belief, the Church does not oppose contraception merely because it sees contraception as artificial; in fact, the Church sees other artificial means, such as manufactured drugs and food that help the body grow and function, as proper. NFP avoids pregnancy by not engaging in sex, the very act that leads to pregnancy, during periods of fertility. Contraception, on the other hand, interferes with the very nature of the sex act—either by blocking the act, preventing ovulation, or killing the sperm. With NFP, the couple is choosing not to act. With contraception, they are actively doing something to prevent conception. Philosophically, they are very different. There is no moral obligation for a couple to have sex on any particular day. Not acting in that circumstance is not immoral. Saying "no" when a spouse is ill is actually considered a loving act. On the flip side, the *Catechism of the Catholic Church* states that contraception is intrinsically evil.[23]

Don't be confused, however; this does not mean that the Church advocates infrequent sex in marriage. It encourages couples to be open to life and only to resort to periodic abstaining when necessary. It does not say, "Try NFP as birth control, but if it doesn't prevent pregnancy, then resort to contraception." It says, "If need be, resort to abstinence when you must."

## Why NFP?

My wife and I have been married and have practiced NFP for four years. We firmly believe that it has tremendous benefits for our marriage. Here are just a few of the reasons why we have made this choice. NFP helps to make sure that we are always loving one another and giving ourselves fully to each other in sex. Periodic abstinence—which NFP requires for those spacing their children—helps to keep our sex life fresh and exciting. Since we are forced to relate in other ways during those times, when we are able to relate sexually it has a deeper context in our entire relationship. It's like another honeymoon at times. There are many times when our sex has been spontaneous, flowing out of our relationship, which is great. Yet NFP prevents us from using each other to meet our own needs. It is the only means of birth control that requires communication, an essential ingredient to good marriages. We are guaranteed that our children will be conceived in love and never "an accident" or "a mistake," as we are open to conceiving every time we have sex.

One of the best, though perhaps the most difficult, reasons for using NFP is that it requires us to trust in God. It can be hard not to be fully in control, but God asks us to trust that his plan is good. If we believe that God loves us, then we also believe that he would not do anything to us that would be ultimately destructive. When we let God be in control, though, we can have confidence that nothing he gives us will be too much for us to bear with his grace. When we choose chastity prior to marriage, it is a lot easier to trust in God and choose NFP within marriage.

When James and Joanne were first married, they decided to use the pill for birth control. Initially, their decision was made because it seemed convenient, and lots of people were doing the same thing. Their friends Kevin and Angie chose to use condoms. After their first years of marriage, both couples began to experience dissatisfaction with the choices they had made to contracept. They investigated NFP and decided to try it. As a result, both couples have experienced a deeper satisfaction in their relationships, freedom from the negative consequences of contraception they were experiencing, and a greater respect for their own procreative abilities. Even after one of the couples has had two children and the other three, both couples adamantly resist any suggestion of returning to contraception.

Chastity respects the importance and power of sex. It recognizes the dual purpose of sex as procreative and unitive. Contraception violates both of these purposes. Complete unity can never be obtained by successive acts of incomplete union. Just as premarital sex dulls the levels of intimacy, so does contraception. Contraception kills the complete gift of sex. In marriage it ruins sex slowly by separating the life-giving purpose of sex from the marital act. Manipulating sex, whether in marriage or out of marriage, to be something it is not kills the power, depth, and beauty of sex.

# Laying Aside a Myth

. . . . . . . . . . .

## Doesn't Chastity Lead to Repression?

God is not a kill-joy. If God wanted to ruin all our fun, the Bible would include the following commandments:

11. Thou shall not whitewater raft;
12. Thou shall not bungee jump;
13. Thou shall not ride a roller coaster.

God actually wants us to experience joyous fun. God, who created sex, knows that it is pleasurable. God could have made sex dull and boring, but he didn't. And God did not create sex to be good for some people and bad for others; God wants it to be good for everyone!

So why did God create something as enjoyable and pleasurable as sex, only to deny us the opportunity of indulging in it before marriage? If it is so good, why can't we have it when we want to? Sex, like any other human desire or function, has a clear purpose, time, and place.

### Sex As Natural Desire

Our sexuality is a natural part of who we are, and sexual desire is a natural part of our sexuality. We can be sexually attractive and have a sexual desire for many people, but the natural use of our sexual arousal and completion is to unite ourselves fully with another person and procreate. It can seem repressive not to act on our natural desires. However, there are appropriate and satisfying ways to fulfill our natural desires, as well as inappropriate and unsatisfying ways.

To understand this concept, let's look at the natural human desire for food. When we become hungry, our body desires food. When we eat, we usually satisfy that desire, but some ways of eating do not. If we overindulge or eat the wrong foods, we will probably feel unsatisfied. God wants us to eat for nourishment, and he loves it when we enjoy the food we are eating. But that doesn't mean that we can eat anything at anytime we wish. I might smell cinnamon rolls and be starving, desiring to eat the sweet treat. But, if I realize that it's merely a cinnamon candle burning, it wouldn't be wise to satisfy my desire by eating wax. There's a better way to fulfill my desire. Just because sex, like eating, is a human desire, does not mean we can do it anytime, in any place, or with whomever we please.

The natural purpose of sex is to unify two people for life and for procreation. The pleasure and intimacy that comes from sex is what bonds a man and a woman together. This unification is meant to be permanent so that it can welcome the other purpose of sex, a baby. Sex is a beautiful communication intended to bond two people for life—for better or worse, one baby or many. Therefore, it is actually *unnatural* for us to give all of ourselves to whomever we want along life's path. Sex outside of marriage does not satisfy our natural desire for healthy sexual relations. Chastity, however, does. Chastity recognizes and seeks out the natural, created use of our sexuality.

## Repression

Of all our natural desires, it is usually only our sexual desires that are considered repressed when not acted upon. Hunger can lead naturally to a legitimate desire for food. However, if it is the wrong time, place, or food, not acting on that hunger is hardly considered repression. Not spoiling one's dinner with cookies beforehand is not repressive. Similarly, chastity recognizes sexual attraction and desire while discouraging inappropriate fulfillment (lust). Are we repressing our sexual desire by not acting it out? No. Repression is more than not acting out one's desires.

Sexual repression is shutting down or diminishing the strength of one's sexuality. Repression can occur in our thoughts and in our actions. Whenever we try to deny, minimize, or ignore our sexuality, we are repressing. If our view of sex is that it is bad or evil, we are being repressive. The Church teaches that our sexuality—who we are as men and women and sexual beings—is beautiful, unique, and valuable, not only when we are engaging in marital sex but at all other times in our lives. Therefore, sexual repression—attempting to minimize or destroy a gift from God—is the opposite of Church teaching.[24]

## Repression and the Church

If you think the Bible and the Catholic Church view sexual morality as "Just don't do it," "Sex is bad," and "No, no, no," you have a world of incredible discovery ahead of you. Try reading the Old Testament book Song of Solomon. Not only does this book describe attraction and marriage, it details sexual desire and sex in marriage.

Pope John Paul II has made teaching about sex a priority of his papacy. His goal has been to clarify the truth of our sexuality in a world where we often take the extremes—either repression or total liberation. He used his weekly addresses for the first five years of his papacy to make sure Catholics understood how much the Church believes in the beauty and power of sexuality. Through his teachings, the pope consistently advocates chastity as living the fullness of our sexuality, elevating sex, not repressing it.[25]

## Repression: Shutting Down Entirely

Repression can take different forms. The first type views sex as essentially wrong or bad. Whenever we think of sex as so bad that any sexual thought or desire is to be avoided at all costs, we are shutting down our sexuality.

> Although Brandon would never say the words, "sex is bad," every time he had a sexual thought, he'd experience tremendous guilt. Instead of recognizing his thoughts as a natural part of life, he mentally punished himself, attempting to reject the fact he was even created as a sexual being. It took him years into his marriage to finally open up and truly enjoy sex.

## Repression: Shutting Down Before Intercourse

Some groups advocate abstinence only from intercourse but allow anything else up to that point. However, sexual arousal was created for fulfillment, for complete and total union with another. Sexual arousal for the mere purpose of pleasure for the moment is lust, which is far from healthy or chaste. Repeatedly arousing and then stopping before intercourse subconsciously trains our bodies to stop rather than to fulfill the act of sex, leading to repression.

Because it is not healthy or loving to tease and then shut down sexual acts, the Church tells us not to use genital stimulation before marriage. The Church wants us to experience only the natural and profound journey of arousal to fulfillment, nothing less.[26]

## Repression: Shutting Down From Guilt

People who engaged in premarital sexual relationships may later feel guilty about those experiences. They then attach feelings of guilt and shame to sex. When they marry, they may struggle with enjoying sex—it reminds them of hurt from past experiences.

Rebecca, a successful, young professional adult was only "mess-ing around" with her boyfriend, hoping to save sex for marriage. But, they got too close and she became pregnant. Her boyfriend denied the possibility that he was the father. At the time, abortion wasn't legal in the state where she lived, but she thought it was the only option. She traveled two states away to undergo an abortion and suffered severe emotional turmoil for her decision. She kept it a secret from most people who loved her. Rebecca subconsciously associated the guilt of the abortion with the act of sex itself and her decision to indulge in the act. She's been married for many years and has yet to experience true sexual arousal from her spouse.

## Avoiding Repression

Jesus tells us that using someone for our pleasure, even in our minds, is sinful. *"But I say to you that everyone who looks at a woman with lust has already committed adultery with her in his heart"* (Mt 5:28). So how can we respond to a sexual desire or attraction without re-pressing it? We must remember that sexual thoughts or desires for another is natural, especially in relationships. When these occur, we should thank God for the gift of attraction and healthy sexuality. As described in the chapter on "Just My Thoughts" (page 62), we should also keep such thoughts under control to avoid lust. Prayer can help us achieve this response. "The more we invite Christ into our pas-sions and desires and allow Him to purify them, the more we find we're able to exercise proper control of them."[27]

Whenever Heather is tempted to daydream about sexual intimacy or to remember lustful moments of the past, she simply prays the name of "Jesus" as many times as needed until the thoughts are trans-formed into truth. The truth is that sexual desire is natural. The truth is that choosing chastity fulfills our sexuality. The truth is the past has been forgiven.

God's plan never was for us to shut down our sexuality but instead to recognize it always as a gift. To treat it as a gift, we need to learn to avoid or transform tempting situations. Repression on a variety of levels strips us of the fullness and fulfillment of our sexuality. On the other hand, living chastely helps us to avoid repressing this gift by recognizing the value of sex and using it only according to its created, natural purpose.

# MAKING A DISTINCTION
## (BETWEEN HOMOSEXUAL ORIENTATION AND BEHAVIOR)

· · · · · · · · · · · ·

## I Can't Help It; It's Just How I Am

This chapter can be summed up in this statement: While human beings are "animals" (biological classification), they are not "animals" (in terms of their behavior). I, Pete, don't remember much from my sophomore biology class—it was one of my least favorite subjects—but I remember learning that one thing that separates humans from all the other animals is the ability to do higher reasoning. For this chapter, I will focus on two components of higher reasoning, making judgments and using self-control. Both qualities are essential to understanding the Church's teaching on sexuality and homosexual attraction.

Having good judgment is one of the key signs of a mature person. It is the ability to look at a situation, analyze the options, and choose the one that is best. One cannot function as a responsible person in our world without this ability. It is possible to function while repeatedly making bad judgments, but people who do, I think, are probably quite miserable. However, we do not have the option not to judge. My students often get angry when I tell them they cannot avoid judging.

What most people mean when they say we shouldn't judge is that we shouldn't be judgmental. Jesus himself said, *"Do not judge, so that you may not be judged"* (Mt 7:1). Jesus, I'm sure, didn't mean we should not evaluate whether one behavior is better, more kind, or more loving than another. Rather, he was talking about not condemning people for their actions. He did not say that we shouldn't judge whether their actions are good. Morally speaking, we can judge behavior as good or bad, but we aren't to judge the person; that role belongs to God alone.

Some people profess to be judgment-free when it comes to ideas and values. That is, all ideas and all values are equal in merit and worth. (Paradoxically, this is a judgment in its own right.) I am saying the opposite. The sign of a mature adult is the ability to judge which ideas and values have worth and which belong on toilet paper.

A second key sign of a mature person is self-control. This is the ability to refrain from acting on every impulse that comes to mind and body, a characteristic that distinguishes most adults from children. Sadly, many adults do not have this ability. Since I am assuming that most young people wish to become mature adults, it is important for them to develop this self-control.

## Attraction Is Not Behavior

There is a distinction between sexual attraction and sexual behavior. We, as human beings, need not act on every sexual thought or attraction that we have. When I married my wife, I did not promise that I would never be sexually attracted to any other human being. What I did promise was that I would never act on an attraction to another human being. Two logical consequences follow this conclusion.

One, we can be sexual beings without having sex. No one denies that sexuality is a part of who we are. Yes, some people try to deny their sexuality, but psychologically, those people are unhealthy, perhaps repressed. Our genitalia—our physical sexual organs—are not the same as our sexuality—the sexual nature of our being.

Often, the expression of our sexuality is defined as a genital act and a genital act only. Sexuality, however, is expressed in many ways, only one of which is intercourse. Not having sex on a regular basis, or even at all, doesn't contradict our sexual nature. Rather, it means we are simply exercising self-control—not acting on every sexual thought and attraction—which expresses our sexuality as a gift of committed love alone. This is important because many people—perhaps even some parents—expect teenagers to have sex because they think teenagers are incapable of self-control. Personally, I know too many teenagers to think that poorly of them. Sure, some teenagers exhibit no evidence of self-control, but many do.

Two, we can have a sexual orientation without having sex. Our sexual orientation, that is, who and what type of people we are attracted to, is a part of our sexuality. This, as I have said before, can be expressed in ways other than through a genital act. This distinction is key to understanding the Church's teaching on homosexuality, and it contradicts what our culture and society say to us almost every day.

## Homosexual Behavior

Homosexual desires for union are unhealthy because they can never be fulfilled by acting on them. In God's plan of creation, our sexual identity comes from our biology: we are either male or female. As such, we are called to "complete" one another, physically and in other areas as well. Though there are some—priests, sisters, brothers, singles—who give up this natural inclination to be united completely with another human being,[28] we are biologically designed to "fit" with a member of the complementary sex. A man prepares to give when aroused; a woman prepares to receive. It is beautiful and fulfilling. Anything less is outside of God's plan for union. A homosexual union, even if called a "marriage," can never be completed in this way.

## Homosexual Attraction

Homosexual attractions themselves are not immoral. The Catholic Church does not discriminate; it holds all people, regardless of sexual orientation, to the same moral standard for their sexuality. That is, the purpose and role for sex does not change according to one's orientation. The proper place for sex is in a sacramental marriage between a man and a woman. Whether we are homosexual or heterosexual, we are called to chastity, which respects our sexuality so much that we participate in sex only in marriage.

There are many who will claim that homosexual attraction is a completely genetic phenomenon, much like eye color or left-handedness,[29] that is, it cannot be helped and therefore acting on those attractions is acceptable, or moral. While there are people who are thoroughly convinced of this, there is no clear evidence that supports the fact that homosexuality is genetic in this way.[30] Even if a person's same-sex attraction was completely genetic, that would not be an excuse to act on the attraction. In different ways, we are all tempted to behave poorly, regardless of our attractions. Heather, for example, may never marry, but is strongly attracted to men. If God doesn't call her to marriage, this attraction is a cross she will have to bear for life; but it is worth it for the sake of real love, the kind of love that ultimately wants the best for everyone.

Our culture has developed, over the past forty years, a "who cares?" attitude toward sex. Visual images once reserved for R-rated movies can now be seen in some TV commercials. In this social climate, homosexuality has not only become acceptable behavior but also an issue of tolerance. Those who do not accept this behavior have been called intolerant, hatemongers, ultraconservatives, or even homophobic. True, some who oppose homosexuality do treat others poorly. But opposing homosexuality can be opposition to behavior, much like opposition to drug use, rather than to personal characteristics or qualities, which would be more like discrimination on the basis of race or gender.

At the same time, our culture has adopted a relativistic understanding of morality. Moral relativism denies the existence of objective truth and holds that determining right and wrong can only be done in the context of the people involved, the situation, and a myriad of other social and personal factors. While this book is not the place for an in-depth look at moral relativism, we can acknowledge that moral relativism affects the way our society views sex. The difficulty with being a moral relativist is that objective norms for our behavior do, in fact, exist. Can you think of a situation in which rape would be morally acceptable? I cannot. If objective norms exist, then we can apply them to behaviors (ours and others), and judge appropriately whether the acts are moral or immoral.

It is wrong to be intolerant of people, to hate them, and to be closed to loving others who are different from us. BUT it is not wrong to judge behavior as unacceptable or immoral. It is not wrong to look at a behavior and judge that it is unhealthy. It is not wrong to say that an immoral action for me is also an immoral action for you.

We know and love many people who are choosing a homosexual lifestyle. But we also know that true peace, freedom, and love comes from God's plan for our fulfillment. For those who struggle with same-sex attractions and living chastely, listen to this message from Cardinal Francis George, Archbishop of Chicago, given in an address to the National Association of Catholic Diocesan Lesbian and Gay Ministries:

> It is possible, with God's grace, for everyone to live a chaste life, including persons experiencing same-sex attraction. To deny that the power of God's grace enables those with homosexual attractions to live chastely is to deny, effectively, that Jesus has risen from the dead.[31]

There are resources and organizations available for those with same-sex attractions seeking to live chastely. Check out Appendix A (page 157) for a list of some of them.

> When Andy was in junior high, a number of high-school students in his neighborhood befriended him. Andy, who was often ridiculed at school, found acceptance from this group of guys. Soon, however, Andy's friends introduced him to the homosexual lifestyle. Because of these experiences, Andy began to think of himself as gay and began to experience sexual attraction for other guys. During his junior year of college, Andy began to practice chastity—refraining from sex and sexual encounters. In choosing chastity, Andy began to explore some of the reasons for his behavior. He learned that his homosexual attractions developed from his experiences and behaviors. As a result, he underwent counseling to help him deal with the hurt and rejection that was the source of many of his unhealthy behaviors.

More than any other moral issue, homosexuality requires a delicate response. It is difficult for people to hear "I accept you, but I don't accept your behavior." Many people have been led to believe that accepting me means accepting my behavior. In the gospels, the Pharisees confront Jesus with a woman who was caught in adultery (Jn 8:2–11). Much is made of the many aspects of this story, but I will touch upon two things. First, Jesus cares for this woman and shows her tremendous respect and love. He truly accepts her. Second, he calls her behavior sinful. Sometimes we are really good at one aspect of our actions and not so good with the other.

The Church's teachings about many things are difficult because they contradict what society and culture tell us. It is a challenge to support and live ideas that are truly countercultural. However, recognizing the distinction between our sexual desires and our sexual behaviors empowers us to embrace chastity with the fullest respect for our sexuality.

# Nobody But Me

· · · · · · · · · · ·

## What's the Big Deal With Masturbation?

The sexual drive, especially in young people, is extremely strong and frequently seems to demand immediate gratification. No surprise there, I'm sure. Many people understand the Church's teaching on premarital sex and commit to saving their sexuality for marriage. At the same time, they struggle with what to do with this strong sexual drive that demands attention. Inevitably, the question of masturbation arises. Students ask, "Isn't it okay to satisfy one's sexual desires personally?" "No one is being harmed by it." "It's not sex with anyone, so why does it matter?"

Chastity means respecting our sexuality, and masturbation violates this respect. Six key reasons explain why masturbation disrespects and even damages the gift of our sexuality.

First, masturbation never fulfills the purpose for sex. Chastity is respecting our sexuality so much so that we reserve it for the context of marital love. Masturbation thwarts that respect. What is created to be a gift for another is not to be a treasure hoarded for oneself. When someone masturbates, he or she is taking for himself or herself what should be given to another. No giving is involved. The twofold purpose of sex—to be life giving and love giving—is denied by the act. It is neither loving another nor giving life to another or to a relationship.

Second, masturbation fails to satisfy the person engaging in it. Many people argue that masturbation is necessary, especially for teenagers, to help to control the sexual drive. They claim that the urges that arise are too strong to do otherwise. The problem with this view is that masturbation, while temporarily relieving sexual tension, actually has the long-term effect of increasing sexual desires. An analogy that can be applied here is that sexual desires can be compared to a two-year-old child. If you say "yes" to a two-year-old when he or she asks you to do something or to give him or her something, soon the child is asking for something else. The more the child hears "yes," the more the child receives "on request," the more the child demands. If, however, the child hears the word "no," eventually the frequency of the demands lessen. So it is with our sexual urges. Attempting to satisfy them by masturbating does not lessen them; rather, it increases their strength and the frequency with which they demand attention. The more one masturbates, the more one will feel the need to masturbate.

Third, built-up sexual desire isn't fatal. No man has died from too much sperm production. No woman has died from not masturbating. God, the designer of our bodies, has not left us to fight a losing battle. For men, our bodies have a natural means of releasing sperm through wet dreams or nocturnal emissions. There is nothing immoral about this natural process, but rather it is a sign of a healthy sexuality. This does not mean, as some might suggest, that it is acceptable to help the natural process along.

Fourth, chastity is a mastering of our impulses and desires, not a submission to them. Masturbation as a means of dealing with our sexual desires makes us a slave to them rather than the master over them. The sexual urge is aroused and demands attention. It is dealt with by masturbating. The sexual desire is having its way. Who is in control? Some would argue that the person is still in control and just has the same aim or goal as the sexual desire. This may be the case for some people, at least initially. However, masturbation can be a highly addictive behavior. Many people start masturbating regularly in high school as a release and end up with a compulsive behavior that they can't stop even ten or fifteen years later. The more one feeds the desire, the stronger the desire becomes and the less able one is to control it. It doesn't take long to become a slave to one's sexual desires.

Fifth, masturbation trains us to achieve arousal by our own hand. Trained in this way, our spouse may not measure up or satisfy us as well. This would be a sad statement about our sexuality if we brought greater physical fulfillment to ourselves than our spouse did.

Sixth, masturbation has negative effects on our relationships. Our sexuality is meant to be expressed sexually in the context of a relationship. Instead of a loving focus on another, masturbation turns sex into a self-focused action. As one friend puts it, masturbation is a monologue rather than a dialogue.[32] Sexual acts are meant to be a dialogue. The self-centered tendencies of masturbation affect our lives—relationally and spiritually. The more we focus on our own selves, the less we are able to give fully to others. Self-centeredness, in all its forms, keeps us from loving others with a deep and real love. Masturbation trains us to use sex for selfish reasons, and it is this training that has a negative effect on our ability to experience sex as fully loving another. The great gift of sexuality that is preserved through chastity is weakened through masturbation.

## Resisting Temptation

All this being said, understanding the Church's opposition to masturbation may not help us deal with the temptations to masturbate. While masturbation is objectively wrong and immoral, factors are present that affect our own moral responsibility—especially if it has become a habitual compulsion. This is why the Church offers us the sacrament of reconciliation.[33] Frequent experiences of the sacrament provide us with both forgiveness for our past sins and grace to avoid sin in the future. Once we sin in the area of sexuality, the easier it becomes to commit that sin again. Reconciliation breaks that cycle and restores us to wholeness, allowing us to start again. Reconciliation is not an instant cure for any habitual sin, including masturbation.

Rather, what we need is a renewal of our minds, and the sacraments can help us to do this. If we combine the sacraments with spiritual direction from someone, perhaps our confessor, we can better determine our weaknesses and more fully accept God's grace in moments of temptation.

Several other steps can help to increase one's ability to resist the temptation to masturbate. As we discussed in an earlier chapter, the temptation to masturbate can come from an unhealthy thought life. One means of lessening the temptation is to foster a healthy thought life. This includes guarding what we watch and appropriately dealing with sexual thoughts.[34]

A second means is prayer. It is difficult to be deep in prayer and commit a sinful action simultaneously. However, we rarely jump into deep prayer from nothing; we have to work our way there with consistent and regular communication with God. One powerful prayer that can transform us, especially in the area of our sexuality, is the rosary.

A third means is having some form of accountability in one's life. Whether this is a regular confessor, a youth or prayer group, a close friend, or another spiritual resource, having another person who regularly offers encouragement and support can be a big help in overcoming regular temptation.

A fourth means is recognizing that there are other ways to release sexual energy—through exercise, for example—that can keep our sexual desires in a more healthy balance.

A final means of overcoming the temptation is greater self-awareness. This means recognizing that masturbation has many causes, including lust. Stress, loneliness, fear, hurt, rejection, and separation from God are all elements that can contribute to our inability to resist temptation. The greater our self-awareness, the better able we are to reduce the influence of these factors.

Remember, temptation should never be confused with sin. Being tempted to masturbate is simply being tempted. Jesus himself was tempted in all ways, yet he did not sin.[35] Jesus desires us to be pure and to be whole sexually. To be so, we have a tremendous amount of grace available to us to overcome the temptations that we encounter.

Mark had never heard from his Catholic schooling that masturbation was an unhealthy behavior. Many people explained it as simply a phase that most guys experience—not a big deal. Yet Mark knew something wasn't quite right. He felt very selfish and especially lonely in the act. In addition, it became an addiction for him. After a retreat during his freshman year of high school, on his own, Mark realized that his practice of masturbating wasn't part of God's plan for his sexuality, and it was distancing him from God. Mark began praying seriously for freedom from masturbation. Although it took time, with God's help, he is no longer a slave to masturbation. As a senior in high school, Mark enjoyed a deep relationship with his girlfriend, a relationship in which they both cherished chastity. After he graduated, he even returned to talk to the freshmen guys at his high school, so they wouldn't get trapped in such a selfish act either.

# ORAL SEX

. . . . . . . . . . . .

## Is It Really Sex?

Yes! Oral sex is sex. Because of its sexually arousing nature, oral sex—just like dry sex, manual sex, phone sex, and cybersex—appropriately carries the title of sex. Is it intercourse? No. Biologically, that should be obvious. Since it is not intercourse and one technically does not lose his or her "virginity," many teens and preteens view oral sex as the best way to avoid the consequences that intercourse brings—both emotional and physical repercussions.

> Scott, fifteen, reported that he hadn't had oral sex, but he would
> like to. He said, "Me and my friends don't think of it as a really big
> deal. I guess, you know, it's less chance of disease and pregnancy,
> and it feels good. With oral sex, it's really quick and less serious
> [than intercourse]. And you don't really have to like the girl."[36]

## A Less Serious Act?

Is oral sex really less serious? In some ways, yes. It is obviously less serious than intercourse insofar as pregnancy is concerned. Although oral sex alone cannot cause pregnancy, one is still susceptible to contracting almost every STD, including HIV and HPV. The risk of contracting an STD is present and very real.[37]

From an exclusively physical standpoint, oral sex may not be as "dangerous" as intercourse, but in other ways it is just as serious. From an emotional standpoint, oral sex is much closer to intercourse than it is to kissing. Because of the physically vulnerable nature of the act, oral sex has the potential to be just as emotionally bonding as intercourse, putting one at risk of all the consequences described in the chapter on "Discovering the Unavoidable Consequences of Sex" (page 19). Men and women can keep the title "virgin" while engaging in oral sex, but they miss out on the benefits of a truly chaste life, including all the freedoms described in the chapter on "Freedom" (page 33).

## No Big Deal

Most adults and even older teens are shocked to hear about twelve-year-olds engaging in oral sex, especially in public venues such as bathrooms or with others watching. How can they do this? Because, as Scott described on the previous page, it's not "a really big deal." Yet this mentality is exactly why oral sex, especially at a young age, is damaging and unchaste. Chastity is the virtue that believes all sexual acts are meaningful and are a very big deal.

As with intercourse, the always present and most damaging consequence of oral sex is that it devalues sexual activity. For an individual or for the general preteen culture to think of oral sex as "no big deal" means that the person or culture has stripped sexual intimacy of its bonding power and meaning. Oral stimulation, appropriate in marriage as foreplay to intercourse, is meant to be one of the most private and intimate of all acts. It is a big deal and, therefore, a huge offense against chastity and purity when done outside of marriage. If we decrease the value and meaning of oral stimulation to the point of being "no big deal," what power does a normal kiss have? How pointless do handholding and hugs become? In terms of the marital bed, instead of being a meaningful gift to one's spouse that leads to intercourse, oral stimulation becomes just something already done with many others. Also, a young person who believes oral sex is no big deal will find it much easier to say to themselves,

"Oral sex didn't seem to be that bad, so why not take it a step further. I've already gone this far."

## You Don't Have to Like Each Other?

Andrea was the most intelligent girl in my (Heather's) class. She wasn't cute, funny, or outgoing, but she had the right answers for the history tests. Those of us in the fifth-grade popular crowd showed Andrea a little attention around test time. When it was back to class as normal, we hardly knew she existed. We didn't need to like Andrea; we just used her. And she let us.

Many teens, especially girls, who engage in oral sex are like Andrea. They get attention, perhaps popularity, for doing it. Popularity, however, is different from respect. Being respectable means that one is worthy of honor and esteem. How honorable is it to be used, especially when those using you don't even like you? Often, oral sex requires a person who desires to exploit another and also requires the willingness of the one being used. Teens who allow themselves to be used not only demonstrate a lack of respect for the gift of sexuality but also for themselves. If we do not believe we are worthy of respect, many people will unfortunately take advantage of us.

> As a sophomore in high school, Dan expressed a real concern for some of his female friends. "I'm really worried about them. They give blow jobs all the time. It's sad that they don't have any self-respect."

## Is Oral Sex Appropriate Affection?

It is important to acknowledge that oral sex is purposeful sexual stimulation. As such, it goes beyond affection into the area of lust; its purpose is one's own fulfillment, not the act of giving to another.

Oral sex categorically goes past the breaking point. It arouses another only to disappoint that person by withholding the complete, committed gift that marital intercourse provides. It is ultimately repressive. The context of a dating or even a seriously committed relationship, like engagement, does not turn oral sex into a chaste activity.

## It Feels Good

Instead of seeking popularity, some men and women simply enjoy oral sex for personal pleasure. Yes, oral sex does feel very good; Scott is correct in this assertion. The selfishness this act breeds, however, can grow to a level that makes self-giving sex nearly impossible in the future. If we start engaging in such acts as oral sex, especially at a young age, sex becomes oriented on "me getting off," a mentality that will certainly damage marital sex and intimacy. Even if it's consensual and mutually given, using another to get off before marriage is far from true love. Does training ourselves for anything other than real love make a few moments of stimulation worth it?

> Evan used his good looks to get whatever he wanted—a date with the most popular girl in school, popularity with the guys, and oral sex in all his relationships, both short-term and lengthy. It felt good physically, but after a while he wasn't especially proud of himself. Sure, he was considered "the stud," but emptiness grew within him. Deep down he yearned for real love and respect, but he didn't know how to get it until he started living chastely. After a commitment to chastity, he stopped dating for a while to focus on friendships with girls and to learn more about true respect and honor. Today he remembers oral sexual encounters as moments of shallow pleasure. In his current dating relationship, he refuses to bring himself or the woman he loves to such a place.

# PORNOGRAPHY

## How Does Looking at Pictures Hurt Anyone?

Even as late as the mid nineties, pornography was an isolated danger. Most guys growing up probably knew one or two grade-school friends whose fathers subscribed to *Playboy* magazine. Maybe another guy had a stash of magazines under his bed that his friends would look at when they came over. In contrast, teenagers today can use the Internet to access countless pornography sites. There is no need to obtain pornographic magazines since even hardcore pornography can now be retrieved easily online. With all this access, many teenagers are finding out that very little is more dangerous to living chastely than pornography.

Pornography is any sexually explicit material—stories, photographs, movies, songs, or objects—that is used for or causes arousal. The majority of pornography is targeted toward men who are more easily aroused or stimulated by visual images, although a large number of women also find themselves attracted to pornography.

For purposes of discussion, pornography is divided into two types, soft- and hard-core. Soft pornography consists of revealing pictures of the human body, usually women. Hard-core pornography goes beyond a simple lesson in human anatomy, it is a handbook for every conceivable sexual act, lewd and perverted included. (If you started to list them in your head, please stop; it is unhealthy for you.) Both types are dangerous for several reasons. To simplify the explanations, viewers of pornography will be described as male, and the pornographic image as female.

First, the use of pornography substitutes fantasy for reality. Pornography involves two types of fantasy. One type of fantasy deals with the actual material or person(s) displayed in the pornography. Because there is no relationship, the person displayed becomes an object, a thing, used to satisfy the viewer's desires. Though she might resemble a woman, she is not a real woman with desires, wishes, preferences, opinions, ideas, thoughts, feelings—she is always just an object to viewers.

Another, and second, type of fantasy deals with the thoughts of the viewer. With rare exceptions, the viewer of pornography has no interpersonal relationship with the person pictured. Any sexual arousal that results is outside the context of a committed relationship. The viewer imagines that the picture is a person who is being vulnerable with him. The viewer must create the fantasy of having a relationship with the woman. He must imagine that her vulnerability goes beyond simply showing herself naked and includes physical contact and perhaps sexual vulnerability. In reality, she is not. Vulnerability and intimacy do not exist in this context.

Second, pornography affects how we view our sexuality. What enters our minds affects the way we think. Men, if we spend hours looking at naked women, it is difficult to look at real women and not wonder what they look like without clothes, or what it would be like to have sex with them. Similarly, if we spend hours looking at bizarre sexual acts, we will come to think of those bizarre acts as the norm. Instead of seeing sex as the intimate union of husband and wife—a physical sign of the self-giving love they share—pornography presents sex as arousal and self-gratification. Pornography always switches the sexual focus from the other to oneself. This self-seeking view of sexuality is a distortion of the view that sex is a sacramental act within marriage. The difference is significant. Pornography can change our view of sex from that of total vulnerability—intellectually, emotionally, and spiritually—to one that is strictly physical.

Third, pornography is addictive. Pornography and its accompanying arousal are like eating hot sauce. If we use a mild hot sauce regularly, we will eventually get so used to it that it no longer has the same ability to flavor our food as before. So we will use a hotter sauce until we become used to it. Then we will move on to an even hotter one. Pornography has the same effect. What was arousing yesterday is not today, and the viewer needs more of it or something different. Most people who view hard-core pornography did not start looking at pornography with the most graphic and sexually explicit images. Rather, they started with soft porn, and when that eventually failed to arouse or satisfy, they moved on to more hard-core images. As we stated earlier, the sexual drive is not satisfied by feeding the sexual appetite. Pornography works in much the same manner. Viewing it does not satisfy the appetite, but increases it. This sets the stage for addiction.[38]

Fourth, pornography exploits sexuality for the purpose of profit. It especially exploits the women who are photographed; their bodies and their sexual vulnerability are turned from a gift for their spouse into a commercial product. Exploitation exists even if someone agrees to pose. All women are exploited by pornography, and many women find pornography highly objectionable. Pornography presents an image of physical—sexual—beauty and perfection. Often pictures are airbrushed and adjusted for imperfections. It is easy to think that what we see in pornography is what we can expect in our girlfriend or spouse. Women do not need another reason to focus on their bodies and worry about their appearance.

> Dawn often struggled with her self-image growing up. She was not a size three, so she felt that she did not meet society's definition of beautiful. When she fell in love and married her husband, she experienced love and acceptance from him. Afterwards, she discovered her husband had an addiction to pornography, something that began when he was in high school. This discovery absolutely devastated her, and her self-esteem plummeted.

> She asked, "Why did he look elsewhere? Will I ever be enough?"
> She is unable to be confident in sex; her husband tries, yet often
> fails, to treat her as more than an object during sex. As a result,
> their marriage has been severely shaken.

The previous example shows that pornography ultimately devalues sex and opposes chastity. Marital sex is not what they show in movies; more depth exists in reality. Chastity respects our sexuality. Pornography violates chastity because it removes our sexuality from the world of interpersonal relationships and replaces our partner with an object. The use of pornography is often coupled with the practice of masturbation, which also leads to a devaluing of our sexuality. Instead of a self-giving love as the foundation for sexual activity, self-seeking arousal and pleasure become the drives. As such, pornography destroys our ability to have intense, passionate sex.

> Tim became involved in pornography as a seventh grader. It
> began with curiosity and Internet access and grew into a daily
> compulsion for him. When he was a sophomore in high school
> he attended his cousin's wedding. His cousin and his cousin's
> fiancé had chosen chastity in their relationship. When Tim saw
> the true love between a husband and wife exhibited in a good
> marriage, he recognized his own involvement in pornography
> as a cheap substitute. It was the wake-up call he needed to stop
> his habit and choose a more complete commitment to chastity
> for himself.

# QUESTIONING THE CHURCH

· · · · · · · · · · · ·

## What Do Celibate Men Know About Sex Anyway?

Two issues are present in this frequently expressed criticism of the Church contained in this chapter heading. The first issue is whether we should listen to the Church. The second issue is whether the Church knows anything about sex and human sexuality. Both questions should be answered in the affirmative.

It is a misperception to think that one must either listen to the Church or think for oneself. Ultimately, we all must make our own decisions and live with the consequences—good and bad. Yet, we don't live in a vacuum; we are constantly bombarded with images and messages of all kinds and cannot avoid being influenced by media, friends, other people, and our own experiences as well. The question is not whether we should listen to anyone else in making our own decisions but rather to whom should we listen.

## Conscience

All baptized Catholics are called to live two very important moral principles. Warning: READ BOTH PRINCIPLES. The first is that we are obligated at all times to follow our conscience. When we fail to do so, we sin, which separates us from God until we reconcile with him, primarily through the sacrament of reconciliation. You may be thinking, "Cool!" My conscience tells me that sex is OK if I love this person or that viewing pornography isn't harmful. Therefore, I'm obligated to follow my conscience. It doesn't work that way, because the second principal is equally important. We must form our conscience.

This means that in all circumstances we must seek the truth, especially the truth that the Church teaches. It also means that not knowing something is wrong is not a good excuse if we could have known. Not paying attention in religion class is very dangerous; you could miss something that you will not be able to claim ignorance about later.

Simply following our conscience alone is not enough. First, our conscience may be misinformed. A number of well-meaning people will tell us things that aren't true. They may even tell us that the Church teaches certain things, when, in reality, the Church does not. Probably very few people deliberately try to deceive young people, but people who are misinformed themselves often pass that misinformation along to others. Second, we may have a lax conscience; we may have convinced or deceived ourselves into thinking that a certain objectively wrong action is acceptable. Ideally, our conscience is designed to let us know when we've sinned. However, sometimes we sin a lot and become comfortable with that sin; our conscience then becomes less bothered by those sinful acts. This situation is unhealthy and a major reason for receiving reconciliation regularly; the sacrament helps to keep our conscience sharp.

Since we are obliged to form our conscience, who should we listen to? Teenagers are one of the most highly targeted advertising markets; merchants want their share of the money teens have to spend. In the area of sexuality, many people are getting rich because people are having sex outside of marriage and viewing pornography. The market for contraception and abortion exists because people who are not married are having sex and aren't in a position to bring a child into the world, the natural consequence of their sexual behavior. What do these voices say? They encourage teens and others to "express your sexuality," to "throw off old-fashioned values," to be "liberated," to "ignore the Church" and "think for yourself." These sweet-sounding voices do not have our best interests in mind. The voice of the Church, on the other hand, often sounds harsh. The

Church often says "no" or "wait." These words can be difficult to hear, especially when other voices are easier to follow. So why should we listen to the Church? Many reasons exist, but they can be grouped into the three key reasons that are given in the following sections.

## Tradition

Jesus taught his followers many things about life and about God. These men and women received the gift of the Holy Spirit which enabled them, among other things, to remember the things that Jesus said and did (Jn 14:26). The apostles handed on that teaching through their own words and writings; God's word passed on in the hearts of the faithful (Tradition) and the writings that became the Bible (Scriptures) are the sources of the Catholic faith. In every contemporary and historical issue affecting humanity, the Church has attempted to teach faithfully what Jesus taught.

Since the time of the apostles, the Church has taught consistently that the appropriate place for sex is in marriage and that we are called to pursue the virtue of chastity. The Church has espoused this position because it has understood this to be the teaching of Jesus, of God. God knows about sex because God created it, and it is his gift to us. He has left us the "owner's manual" for sex through his teachings that come to us through Tradition and through Scripture.

## Wisdom of Collective Human Experience

The Church has existed for two millennia and has learned much from the experience of the people who have belonged to it. A key sign of maturity is to be able to learn from someone else's mistakes as well as from one's own. A person doesn't have to be hit by a truck to know that this collision would hurt. Listening to the wisdom of the Church allows us to take advantage of mistakes made by others.

Priests and bishops, men who may or may not have experienced sex, have tremendous insight into human nature. In the confessional, people have poured out their hearts and the truth of their experiences in ways they rarely do with any other human being. Priests see and hear firsthand the damage and pain that occurs when people use their sexuality in unchaste ways. This deep understanding of people has led the Church to affirm more strongly its teaching on sexuality.

The teachings of Jesus and of the Church center around God's love for us in the person of Jesus and in the Eucharist. The moral teachings of the Church center around our efforts to live lives that reflect this love. Priests and bishops, through their devotion to the Eucharist and their practice of celibacy, have insight into the self-sacrificing love of Christ himself. This view is not one of love formed by self-interest, popular culture, or media; rather, it is an understanding of love that comes directly from God, the source of love.

Many cultures have come and gone since the Church began. Some were vast empires that covered most of the known world; today these places are simply archaeological sites or historical footnotes. During all that time, the Church has consistently taught the same values and understanding of sex. People who have chosen chastity and the cultures that have fostered it have experienced the positive consequences of the right use of sexuality and avoided the negative consequences of promiscuity.

## Church Teachings Protect and Provide for Us

The Church's experience of God, especially through the person of Jesus, is that he loves us absolutely and completely. God only wants good for us and for our lives. When the Church teaches that we should practice chastity, it is not to enslave us or to limit our fun, but rather because the Church wants the best for us.

A friend frequently uses a great analogy. A hamster who lives in a cage is always trying to do one thing—get out of the cage. It can see a whole world through the bars and wants to get out and explore that world. The owner, however, knows that the hamster is better off inside the cage. The hamster doesn't see what the owner knows; a drooling cat is waiting for the hamster to get out of the cage. What the hamster sees as a prison is actually a home. The owner knows that the cage protects the hamster from harm. The owner also provides everything else the hamster needs, namely food and water.

The boundaries given to us by the Church are like the hamster's cage. They protect us from things, often unknown to us, that can harm us. They also provide us with good things that we need and want, even if we aren't sure that we need or want them. In terms of sex, chastity protects us from all of the negative physical, emotional, and spiritual consequences that come from having sex outside of marriage. God and the Church know the harm that comes from misusing our sexuality and want to protect us. God and the Church also know that chastity provides us with a means to learn to love someone fully, to be loved fully, to experience a marriage that is full of joy and blessings, and to live truly free.

Kris was a typical teenager in high school. He didn't see much use for the Church and its teachings and challenged them in religion class whenever he could. It wasn't that he didn't believe in God or didn't see the value of saying a prayer every so often; he simply didn't think the Church should be interfering in people's lives. During his senior year, he had sex with his girlfriend; she had thought it might mend some problems they were having. As Kris says, "My first time might sound great, but it wasn't. I was drunk, and it was with a girl I didn't even love." This experience helped Kris to be more open to what the Church has to say about sexuality.

The Church has been given the charge to teach faithfully what Jesus taught. Even if everyone else in the world is doing things differently, the Church cannot change what it teaches when those teachings have come from Jesus. Listening to the Church as we form our conscience helps us to avoid both a misinformed and a lax conscience. It is hard to deceive ourselves when we honestly seek sources of truth outside of ourselves.

In the end, no one forces us to act a certain way. Even the Church recognizes and supports our questioning, doubts, and ultimate freedom of choice. The Church attempts to guide us, to speak the truth to us, to help us form our conscience in ways that keep us free from harm and ultimately bring us good. We can choose to listen or not and, in the end, we must live with the results of our choices. We, the authors of this book, really care about you and your happiness and joy in life. We know from our own experiences and from working with thousands of young people that great pain comes from ignoring the Church's teachings regarding sex, and great joy comes in living a life of chastity.

# RESPECT THAT
# BUILDS SELF-ESTEEM

· · · · · · · · ·

## But I Like Attention

We are all created good. God tells us this and reminds us of it. "*For everything created by God is good* (1 Tim 4:4). "*You are precious in my sight, and honored, and I love you*" (Isa 43:4). Yet many of us do not fully believe these words. How we feel about ourselves often pales in comparison to the truth that we are infinitely valuable to God. Throughout our teen years, we might feel inadequate, especially in comparison to peers and entertainment icons. Sometimes we look for quick fixes to boost our self-esteem. However, attention getters such as sexual involvement or relationships outside of marriage fail to make us truly feel better about ourselves. We need true respect to build our self-esteem, not just attention to body parts or one aspect of our personhood. Chastity trains us to give and to receive true respect for the whole person. What we need most is the type of respect that comes from chastity, not from whistles of approval or heavy make-out sessions.

## Self-Esteem

Self-esteem is how we view ourselves at the core of our being. When we are very young, our self-esteem is formed by our parents. By the age of five or six, most of us attend school and are surrounded by other children our age. We begin to look to our peers instead of our parents as the primary source of acceptance. As we grow up, we can be ignored, betrayed, ridiculed, or dumped; often these actions hurt us most deeply when they come from those closest to us. Instead of fulfillment, life offers us disappointment. We are constantly compared to others; our worth seems measured against the gifts, talents, abilities, and achievements of others. It is a wonder that any of us have good self-esteem.

Only our Creator can give us a glimpse of our total value. God determined our worth when he thought us important enough to be conceived with our own unique, creative gifts. But God went further and sent us the Savior. Jesus entered our physical world and loved each of us so much—despite how we might hurt, ignore, or betray him—that he died for us.

Deep down we all have a need for love and acceptance. God gave us this need so that we would continually seek a relationship with him. Only his love completes us as it is unconditional and powerful beyond human belief. But, instead of listening to God to find our value, we often look elsewhere. Many of us look to romantic relationships, hoping that we will feel better about ourselves if a member of the complementary sex enjoys our company. Chaste relationships can boost our self-esteem, but unchaste behavior leads to damaged self-esteem.

## Self-Esteem From Sexual Attention

When we receive sexual attention (such as during a make-out session or when a stranger is approvingly checking out our body), we may often feel very good about ourselves. At that moment, we may feel loved, accepted, and sexy. However, when others focus solely on our body parts or on sexual bonding and ignore our emotional, intellectual, and spiritual self, the attention is shallow. Shallow attention never meets our deepest needs to be loved for who we are.

Bridget says, "I always felt that I never measured up. My father and brothers constantly remarked with great awe about the full-breasted, skinny women in public or on television. At football games, my dad would only take out his binoculars for the cheer-leaders. I didn't look like the cheerleaders, so I thought I needed to change. I realized that I needed to wear tight clothing, push up the little chest I had, work out, or do whatever necessary to lose weight so that I could earn male attention. I was not fine just as I was."

Sexual attention separated from a relationship does not tell us that we are good because of who we are. Instead, it tells us that we are worthy of attention because of how we look, how we dress, or what we do. Likewise, we are loved not for who we are but for what we can do. This is not real love, and it fails to satisfy the longings of our hearts and damages our self-esteem. Bridget's self-esteem is based on how physically attractive she believes she is to men. She is not alone. Many adolescent girls have the impression that their body is the most important determinant of their worth. They can easily begin to think, "If I'm not sexy and attractive, I must not be very valuable." While an unhealthy focus on a woman's body is not the sole cause of eating disorders, it certainly is a contributing factor. The more value society places on the physical and sexual attributes of women, the more society must deal with low self-esteem in any girl whose body is not "perfect." On the contrary, chastity requires respect and real love for both our sexual actions and body parts.

Whitney's boyfriend greeted her when he came to pick her up for their date. Before they left the house, he noticed that the shirt she was wearing was very tight and low cut. He asked if she would mind changing into a different top. She was furious, ask-

ing him, "How dare you tell me what to wear!" He responded, "I
know how guys think, and I don't want you to be disrespected in
any way, even in a guy's mind."

## Self-Esteem From Sexual Activity

We go to a very unique place with each other in sex. Our partner sees aspects of us that are hidden from the rest of the world. When we bond physically in such a vulnerable manner, we are being completely accepted by another person, just as we are—skinny, fat, zits on the back, and everything else. Our sexual partner sees all of us, knows us well, and continues to caress, kiss, and fully embrace us. When we're accepted completely in sexual acts, especially intercourse, as part of a caring and emotionally and mentally mature relationship, our self-esteem will rise because we feel accepted and loved.

In marriage, this is powerful in positive ways. Outside of marriage, it is equally powerful, yet this complete acceptance becomes negative. Break-ups are difficult enough in nonsexual relationships. However, if we are rejected after giving ourselves sexually, the pain acts like a bullet to our self-esteem. To be dropped by someone who knows me, but only part of me, is one thing. But to be dropped by someone with whom I have shared such a profoundly vulnerable act is another. It hurts more because my partner is rejecting all of me that he or she once accepted. This is why divorce can be such a self-esteem killer.

Even prior to breaking up, sexual activity can harm one's self-esteem. As we have seen earlier, sex outside of marriage is not a loving act. When people fail to love us fully, our self-esteem suffers. When we attempt to use nonloving actions to satisfy our need to be loved, we are left empty. This emptiness and dissatisfaction may be hidden temporarily, but eventually we will discover the reality. In the long run, our self-esteem is harmed.

## Addiction to Attention and Sex

A vicious cycle can develop when we look to sex to boost our self-esteem. A relationship ends, we experience pain, and our self-esteem drops. We hurt terribly and need to feel better, so we look for affirmation and acceptance through sexual attention, gain it for a while, and then suffer pain and hurt again after the breakup. The following illustrates this cycle:

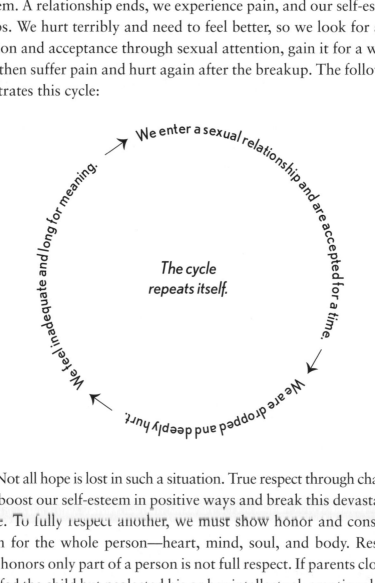

We enter a sexual relationship and are accepted for a time.

We are dropped and deeply hurt.

We feel inadequate and long for meaning.

*The cycle repeats itself.*

Not all hope is lost in such a situation. True respect through chastity can boost our self-esteem in positive ways and break this devastating cycle. To fully respect another, we must show honor and consideration for the whole person—heart, mind, soul, and body. Respect that honors only part of a person is not full respect. If parents clothed and fed the child but neglected his or her intellectual, emotional, and spiritual growth (reading to, hugging, and conversing with them), their parenting would be incomplete.

## Self-Esteem and the Respect of Chastity

Respect for our sexuality is respect for ourselves and for others. Living chastely fosters wisdom to recognize the difference between true and fake respect. Chastity demands real respect and rejects the lie that sexual attention is flattering. It refuses to settle for being used in any way, big or small.

> Angie has been living chastely through her teen years. She has a nice figure and dresses modestly. When a guy came to get Angie for a dance—it was their first date together—he gave her a slow, up-and-down "oh-yeah-baby" look in front of her entire family. Before her brother could punch the guy, Angie gently and politely said, "Please go home." She preferred an evening at home with her family rather than be disrespected by her date, even if it was just in his mind.

> Conner and Jon lived in a fraternity house. During the weekends, their room was packed with good-looking women. Throughout college each of the men dated one or two women seriously. Women on campus loved to hang out with these guys because both of them chose chastity; they were saving sex for marriage. Girls stayed late into the night because they weren't worried that the guys would put "the moves" on them. Women trusted them. Recently, a friend learned that Jon was engaged, and she remarked that Jon's fiancée was one lucky woman! The respect of Jon and Conner was noticed and valued by many.

Because chastity does not settle for disrespect, it invites real love. This love and respect is exactly what we need for authentic and lasting self-esteem boosters.

# Starting Over

. . . . . . . . . . . .

## What If I've Already Lost My Virginity?

Tom didn't live chastely as a teenager. Now in his thirties, he often speaks to teens to let them know about the pain he experienced, the regret he carries, and how freeing life became for him when he stopped having sex before marriage and chose chastity. One of his concerns, however, is that some people consider him a hypocrite. "It affects my witness to other people, some of whom might not listen to me talk about chastity because for some of my life I didn't live it. If, however, I told you that I had once shot myself in the foot, and then encouraged you not to shoot yourself in the foot, I hope you would listen. Why? Because I experienced it—I know the pain firsthand. I promise you—in having sex before I was married, I shot myself in the foot." But more important, Tom often asks those currently not living chastely if they want to continue to shoot themselves in the foot. Today is a good time to start over and begin to experience true healing and freedom. Tom has many regrets from his unchaste decisions but no regrets for choosing chastity.

We all make mistakes. No matter what our past experiences are, we can still choose chastity. Remember that virginity and chastity are not the same. Chastity is not about the past; it's about the present and the future. Whether we've experienced regret or not, whether we've committed major or minor offenses against chastity, we can choose to grow in this virtue from this day forward. People are not destined to alcoholism because they have been drunk once or even ten times. We all have the ability to stop unhealthy behaviors. By choosing chastity now, we can start over. Choosing chastity from this day forward may be very difficult, especially if sex has been part of our lives, but it is possible and worth the challenge. We will gain far more than we will leave behind. "If you've already given away your virginity, do not despair—trust in God's tender mercy...and re-wrap the gift. Sins of impurity cause deep scars, but Jesus can heal all of these. Start over now, and make the decision to persevere in purity."[39]

## The Offer From God

Although God's call to chastity might be challenging, it brings more peace and fulfillment than any plan we can imagine. *"For surely I know the plans I have for you, says the* LORD, *plans for your welfare and not for harm, to give you a future with hope"* (Jer 29:11). His plan for our lives is one that is full of joy, meaning, and love. When we choose to walk away from God, it becomes very difficult to experience the immense love God has for us.

But all is not lost. When we ask for forgiveness, God will forgive us. It doesn't matter what we've done or how much we've sinned, God is willing to forgive us. All we have to do is let God love us. Though none of us are worthy of his mercy, God still bestows it.

As clearly described in the biblical story of the prodigal son (Lk 15:11–32), our heavenly Father literally runs to us when we turn to him and to the plan he has for our lives. After the prodigal son left his father and wasted all his inheritance, he chose to return home and seek forgiveness. Jesus told this story so that each of us would know how God, our Father, responds when we walk back into his plan. He patiently awaits our return and then extravagantly fills us with love and acceptance.

## Turning to God

If we want to grow closer to God and commit to chastity after an unchaste past, it's important to start with forgiveness. Seeking forgiveness from God allows us to take responsibility and begin to put the past behind us. Personal prayer is a simple way to start dialoguing with God again. We can ask for God's help to start over and even to have the courage to humbly ask for forgiveness. Catholics can seek the powerful and merciful sacrament of reconciliation. Through absolution, Jesus (in the form of a priest) whispers in our ears how much he loves us. The cleansing graces we receive in reconciliation make the sacrament a wonderful and necessary experience which helps us commit to chastity and restores our relationship with God. *"So if anyone is in Christ, there is a new creation: everything old has passed away; see, everything has become new!"* (2 Cor 5:17).

Corey (whom we met in the chapter "Attitudes and Approaches," page 1) writes: "I refused to acknowledge this incident anywhere close to the presence of God until a retreat experience at my school almost a year later. I hadn't gone to confession in that entire time. I couldn't. What would the priest think? But during the retreat activities, I felt this need to let it out; I just couldn't fight anymore. God had put me on a retreat, a safe and welcoming environment. He made everything just right. I just had to take the first step.

"I eventually made my way into the confessional that night, and I've never been the same since. I walked out, planted myself under a chair, and felt so overwhelmed that I cried until the tears wouldn't come anymore. God had purged me of all of that pent-up shame and embarrassment and disappointment and guilt and fear. Now, every time I feel afraid to come to God openly and honestly, I remember that night. I remember lying in bed that night with a comfort and joy and relief that I hadn't ever felt before. God lifted from me the burden of regret and shame. I will admit that there are aspects of God and of the Catholic faith that I question from time to time. But one thing I no longer doubt is God's forgiveness and healing—because I've felt it. It's real to me."

Starting over with God does not need to be complex. The sacrifice of Christ on the cross is perfect, and the mercy of God covers all our faults. When we are forgiven, our souls are wiped clean and we are blameless again in the sight of God. Forgiveness, however, is different from escapism. We cannot expect all consequences to disappear because we are forgiven. For example, a teen who contracted a STD might receive God's mercy and healing, but the disease does not disappear. Likewise, our sexual choices have emotional and mental consequences that may linger even after we've made amends to God and others. Therefore, it is important to realize that starting over in living chastely will take more than one prayer or one trip to the sacrament of reconciliation. God can work miracles in our lives with a simple prayer, but we must also be willing to cooperate with grace. Repentance—turning around and walking in the other direction from our sin—must occur for us to receive the fullness of God's mercy. We can't just say, "Thanks, God. Now, I'll go do as I please again." Our ability to receive his mercy and grace is inhibited when we slam the door. However, when we remain close to and trust in God, we can receive the graces necessary to live chastely.

## Making a Commitment

A commitment goes beyond having a strong desire; it means doing whatever is necessary to achieve the goal. Chastity isn't a project we finish or a place at which we arrive. Instead, we can compare it to a journey. Growing in the virtue of chastity requires that we stay on the road of purity and honor. If our car swerves, we quickly try to get back on track. The more we practice, the easier it becomes to stay on the road. Once we've chosen to live chastely, we must tell someone we trust—a mentor, a supportive friend in faith, a priest, or minister. We give this person an opportunity to support and pray for us on the journey. It's also important to choose friends who encourage us in this commitment, such as those in a youth group. Through this time of transition, it is important to find "God in skin." God will give us the support we need through other Christians and friends who uphold the same morals. It will be very difficult for us to be pure if our surroundings are not. For more on living chastely, read the chapters "What to Do" (page 133), "How Can Women Live Chastely" (page 138), and "How Can Men Live Chastely" (page 144).

After choosing not to inflict more pain on others or ourselves with sexual sin, we must now deal with the scars that remain. It is important to learn from our scars and heal them in the best ways possible. Many of us have memories or responses to sex and members of the complementary sex that are far from healthy, holy, and beautiful. The next chapter discusses the healing that is possible with God's grace.

# TRYING TO UNDO THE PAST

## How Can I Move Beyond the Memories?

Although Kayla and her fiancé practiced chastity for many months before their marriage, she carried emotional scars from previous sexual encounters with other men. Regret, pain, and loss had accompanied the breakup of those earlier sexual relationships. Kayla worried that her married sex would drudge up the past—a reminder of the guys with whom she had become so intimate but who had left her. Kayla had been deeply in love with one of her previous boyfriends, and she feared she would remember him at times in which she only wanted to focus on her husband. How could she let go of these memories and joyfully engage in the same activity that had caused her so much hurt?

Jeff experienced casual, meaningless sex. After he made a commitment to chastity, he avoided women. He knew he needed to honor and respect women. But because all of his earlier relationships were based on physical attraction and sexual acts, he had never practiced authentic respect for women. He didn't know how to get close to a woman without wanting to take her to bed. He feared that if he became too close, his old self would take over and he'd repeat his behavior. His past immobilized him from having healthy, freeing relationships with women. How can he move past this?

Both Jeff and Kayla need the same thing: healing. Simply starting over, as the previous chapter describes, only scratches the surface of the transformation that we need and desire. When something deep within us is altered or damaged, we cannot simply ignore the harm to our sexuality or hope it will be all right in the future. If we shoot ourselves in the foot and experience pain, it's a good idea to stop shooting ourselves. That's not the only thing we need to worry about, however; we're still walking around with an injured foot. The foot needs to be restored, and it will take a good surgeon and some medication before it functions as it did in the past. After unchaste sexual experiences, our hearts, minds, and souls also need to be restored because they've been affected or damaged. But restoration takes time and help from the Creator of sexuality, God.

## Misconceptions About "Moving On"

We can move on from an unhealthy sexual past without healing; however, we will not experience the potential fullness of our sexuality as long as it remains contaminated with impurity of the past. Sexual memories do not escape us easily or quickly. To pretend that they disappear is naive. Immediately after the terrorist attack on the World Trade Center on September 11, 2001, if someone had urged us to "move on," that person would have been considered rude. We needed time to refocus on our own values; celebrate and grieve the lives lost; and respond in a positive, healthy manner. Monuments recalling painful events would not be erected and important if all we need to do is simply chalk up hurt, devastation, and pain as learning experiences and "move on."

Many people believe that time, new relationships, and distance can heal all wounds. That is partially true. Time and distance allow us to forget more easily. But for some, the hurt may linger and return when least expected, unless it is dealt with in a healthy manner. Strong, healthy relationships can bring us hope and give us confidence in our ability to maintain good relationships. Often, God sends us people and gives us the time we need to move on more easily. But if we base our healing and strength on a current relationship, what happens if the new relationship ends? What happens if this person betrays us? Further hurt will occur. But even if we find ourselves in an extremely healthy, lifelong relationship, the chance still remains that the memories and hurt can recur years later. The most loving, wonderful, even holy spouse cannot go back to our past and change what took place.

## Real Healing

Nothing can change the past, but healing can transform the "wrong" done either by ourselves or others, into channels of grace and growth. Healing frees us from the negative emotional, mental, and spiritual effects of sexual impurities. With true healing, we can look back with maturity and peace, knowing that our past cannot keep us from real love and freedom. Healing can come in many ways. The more we seek and are open to the types of healing described below, the more likely we will be restored to the person of joy, love, and trust God created us to be.

## Inviting God to Lead the Trip

Healing takes time. "Forgive and forget" sounds nice, but we're human. Even if we experience profound moments of love, forgiveness, peace, and closure from past mistakes, we are rarely able truly to forget. Therefore, our hope in healing is not to shove completely out of our mind all that has happened in the past. On the other hand, true healing allows us to look back on past experiences with compassion, forgiveness, and hope. Emotional and spiritual healing are difficult to obtain with the help and wisdom of other people alone. But if we open ourselves to Jesus, God's healing fills us with unconditional love and forgiveness. Inviting God to heal allows us to experience more than this world, time, or even the most incredible humans can provide.

## Forgiveness

On a retreat, while speaking to eighth-grade girls about their friend-ships, I, Heather, asked Sheila why forgiveness or reconciliation was still lacking between her and Kristen. "She told everyone my secret. It was just so awful—what she did. It was too awful," Sheila replied. Sometimes things do seem too awful for us to forgive. We feel em-powered when we hold on to the anger. Not choosing to forgive, however, is like our drinking poison that we've prepared for the per-son we hate. The other person is rarely affected by our anger.

Although it is difficult to forgive those who hurt us or to seek forgiveness when we've hurt someone else, forgiveness is essential in the healing process. It requires that we take ownership for our ac-tions or our hurt emotions. We must deal with the reality that ac-tions can deeply affect others.

> Wendy was raped as a young teen. She was nothing but polite to this cute guy, but he pushed himself on her. Wendy never saw him again. Does he realize what he did was wrong? Is he sorry? Maybe, maybe not. Has he asked for her forgiveness? No. She had no reason to forgive him for such an awful crime except that she was tired of being bitter. Also, she knew that it was essential. During a retreat she remembered the part of the Gospel when Christ forgives his killers: *"Father, forgive them; for they do not know what they are doing"* (Lk 23:34). While she was praying, she imagined herself climbing up on the cross and looking at the scene of the Crucifixion, picturing the man who raped her in

the crowd. She then said, "I forgive you." Wendy experienced tremendous freedom after that experience. She continues to remember her pain but also continues to forgive the rapist.

## Renewal of the Mind

Jeff was only able to relate well with women after the Holy Spirit transformed his view of sex and women. Our past is in our memory. A random image, song, or book can trigger it. If we watch movies or listen to music with images of shallow sex, our minds will have a difficult time convincing us that chastity is possible or even worth it. We'll revert back to old patterns or only go through the motions of abstaining instead of being able to embrace chastity fully. We all must fill our minds with the truth of how much God loves us. We must remember how beautiful and sacred our bodies and sex are meant to be. Reading the Bible, books on chastity, talking to and surrounding ourselves with strong, wise believers will assist us in this process. Instead of trying to merely throw out lustful thoughts or tendencies, it is best to replace them with healthy and loving truth.

## Human Relationships for Healing

Hal forgave his abusive dad for all the hurt of his childhood and tried to rebuild their relationship. But because of his father's alcoholism, Hal could never get too close, and he had no model of how an honorable father should behave. Hal prayed for healing, and God sent him an incredible Christian man—his father-in-law. While dating his future wife, Hal realized that he could learn much from this new father figure. Through his father-in-law and his relationship with God, Hal received the love of a father which he had never experienced from his own.

Other humans can provide great healing in our lives. When we seek healthy, whole, and healed individuals to be our friends, we are inherently touched by the grace in their lives. To heal after having unhealthy sexual relationships, we must focus on building solid friendships and family relationships. It's important that we be selective in who we seek to help us—not just anyone will do. We need to go to places where strong Christians hang out—at youth groups or church events. God touches us most profoundly, however, through those who allow themselves to be completely filled by him.

## The Divine Relationship for Healing

Through personal or group prayer, sacraments, especially the Eucharist and reconciliation, and retreats, we can be eternally changed. In little or big ways, immediately or over time, we will be healed if we continually open ourselves to God's mercy and love in our lives. God desires to heal all of our painful or shallow experiences. When we are hurt, we can ignore the injury; or we can clean out the wound, apply healing medication, and learn from the experience. When we look at the scars, we don't always need to be reminded of the hurt, but we can be reminded of the healing, hope, and strength we have received. God does not inflict pain upon us but simply hopes that we will allow him to help transform it into something good.

Years after accepting God's gift of a fresh start and much healing, Liz told her new boyfriend about her regretful past. After admitting she was not a virgin, he responded, "It's true, then. The gift of starting over and being healed is real. God can restore a person's purity!" He went on to tell her that he saw her as the most beautiful, holy, spotless, and pure woman that he'd ever known. He said that if her past included anything impure, God had truly healed and restored her.

# UNDER ONE ROOF

· · · · · · · · · · · ·

## What's Wrong With Cohabitation?

Pete relates this story: "During the three years that I was both single and teaching, every year at least one student in each of my classes would ask me if my girlfriend (or fiancée) and I were going to live together before we got married. This happened after we had discussed chastity and sexual morality in class."

For many teenagers and young adults, living together—cohabitation—prior to marriage seems to be as much a part of the engagement as giving or receiving and wearing a diamond ring. Many people think it makes sense. If an engagement is a period of preparation for marriage—the Church encourages preparation for marriage—and married people live in the same house, then living together before marriage should help that preparation. Even as I, Pete, write this, the fallacy in this argument is difficult to see; but more on this later.

Traditionally, married persons were usually and easily identified by shared name, shared home, and shared bed. No so today. Cohabitating couples attempt to live out the traditional marriage elements of shared home and shared bed. The Church clearly teaches—often to the point of denying a Catholic wedding to those who are cohabitating—that living together before marriage is inappropriate and destructive. This can be a hard teaching to understand, and an even harder one to hear if you happen to be a young adult who is living with someone. However, the damage that occurs as a result of cohabitation—both to chastity and to our abilities to enter into Christian marriage—is so destructive that the practice should be strongly discouraged and prohibited.

## Cohabitation: An Impediment to Chastity

If the reason for cohabitation is to make sexual activity easier, the same reasons that make premarital sex harmful make cohabitation harmful. If anything, the negative emotional consequences to premarital sex are greater because living together has the appearance of being more serious than dating, or even of having sex.

For those couples attempting to live chastely, cohabitation only makes it more difficult and challenging. Sharing a home means being alone together regularly, sleeping night after night in the same house, and often using the same bathroom and shower. While it is not impossible to be chaste while cohabiting, the temptations to be unchaste are more frequent and more intense.

## Cohabitation: Unhealthy Dating

For many sexually active couples, cohabitation seems a natural phase of the relationship. After all, if the reason for opposition to living together is that the couple might be tempted to have sex, and they are already choosing to have premarital sex, then there should be no opposition to them living together. However, the consequences of premarital sexual activity aside, even these couples are damaging their relationship by living together.

Cohabitation can distort the reality of the relationship. There is a perceived commitment in living together. This commitment can bind together two people who perhaps should not be together. Much more psychological resolve is needed to leave a cohabiting relationship than to leave a relationship that is simply a dating one. It seems that many people spend too much time stuck in relationships that are unhealthy because they find it difficult to leave. Too often, the difficulty of leaving and the momentum of a progressing relationship lead couples to the altar when they have no business being there. Cohabitation leads many couples to this fate.

If a couple living together does break up, the pain and hurt associated with the rejection is increased. After all, the relationship was serious enough to the point that the couple were living together. If nothing is done, the next relationship will fall into the same trap.

For those couples who are living together and heading for marriage, cohabitation has even more risk. It looks like a marriage, it feels like a marriage, and even has some of the good aspects of marriage—but it is not. What makes marriage good, and even a sacrament, is the total, absolute, and unconditional love professed by the couple. Cohabiting couples have no such profession or commitment.

Psychologically, when cohabiting, a person experiences the freedom to leave at any time. A married person does not share this same psychological freedom. If a married couple has an argument, they have a stake in resolving the dispute. The cohabiting couple does not have the same motivation. When living together, the individuals often overlook their partner's personality quirks, annoying habits, and irritating behavior because they can always leave. When married, these things must be lived with for the rest of one's life. These irritants can have a major impact on the relationship—often in a negative manner.

Cohabitation distorts the reality of marriage. Couples living together can easily be deceived into thinking that what they are doing is "being married" before they are married. They think that once they are married, nothing will change. However, since the commitment for marriage makes a difference in how one views his or her spouse, many couples are surprised to find that things are different after they marry. It is no surprise, then, that couples who cohabit prior to marriage have a higher divorce rate than the general population. Some studies indicate that cohabiting couples are twice as likely than those in the general population to divorce.[40]

Once married, the relationship changes. They no longer have the psychological freedom to leave; and the spouse's personality quirks, annoying habits, and irritating behavior demand more tolerance. This demand for a greater choice of the will, a greater decision to love, is too much for some people. Just as sexually active couples can fall into only relating physically, so can cohabiting couples. It takes more work for them to relate on the intellectual, emotional, and spiritual levels that contribute to healthy dating. The cohabiting couple often have not developed the relational skills they will need in their marriage; the couple has been practicing something else. This is like preparing for an important English test by staying up all night studying vocabulary words, only to have the test focus on the literary merits of *A Tale of Two Cities*. We would all feel totally unprepared.

## Cohabitation: Poor Marriage Preparation

If living together—cohabitation—were the same as marriage, then it might make sense that it could prepare a couple for marriage. Living together before marriage, though, only resembles marriage in the same way that shooting hoops in the driveway resembles playing in the National Basketball Association or dressing up in our parents' clothes when we are young resembles being an adult. Anybody can take a basketball and shoot hoops in the driveway, but not everybody has the skills and abilities to play in the NBA. Dressing like an adult, talking like an adult, and acting like an adult does not make the child an adult; he or she is playing make-believe. Simply put, the couple living together might be doing the same things as married people, they might be practicing some of the skills used by married people, they may even look like and act as though they're married. But they are not married, and this makes a difference.

Marriage involves a publicly professed commitment. The only commitment a couple living together has is to live together until one or the other decides to move out. (Some would argue that marriage has exactly the same commitment; and for some, it might. Most people, however, recognize that marriage involves more than just living together.)

As stated previously, it seems to make sense that a couple experience a trial marriage before they exchange vows. That is the expectation of many cohabiting couples. They say, "We'll live together to see how compatible we are." "We'll live together to see if we should get married." This is equivalent to running two miles every day to determine whether you should enter a marathon. In an attempt to simulate marriage, cohabitation looks similar; but it lacks the requirement that distinguishes marriage from dating and engaged relationships— a publicly professed commitment to faithfulness. It is our choosing to be faithful and committed that determines the marriage relationship, that puts sexual intercourse in the proper context, and that allows for the best upbringing of children. This choice exists in marriage; by definition it cannot exist in a cohabiting relationship.

For those serious about living chastely, living together is not a good choice. For those living together as part of their dating relationship, cohabitation is healthy neither for their relationship nor their potential marriage. And for those living together as preparation for marriage, cohabitation fails to prepare them well. No matter how well-intentioned the reasons may be to cohabit, living together is contrary to God's plan for our dating, sexuality, and marriage. If you want the best marriage and the best sexual relationship in that marriage: don't choose cohabitation.

Kitty and Brett saved not only sex for marriage but also living together. After the honeymoon, they had the adventure of growing sexually together, but they also relished the simple experiences of picking out a mop together and falling asleep in each other's arms. All these new, exciting experiences made the challenges of their first year of marriage more bearable and enjoyable.

# VOCATION OF MARRIAGE

## With So Much Divorce, Is It Really Worth Waiting?

Everyone has probably heard that one-half of all marriages end in divorce. The actual rate is probably lower, between one-quarter and one-third, but even so, the statistics are enough to scare anyone away from permanent commitment. The odds of a successful marriage hardly seem in our favor. Are we attempting to save ourselves for something that isn't worth all that effort? Is a lifetime commitment too much to ask from anyone in today's society? God's answer is clearly NO! God has something special planned for marriage and for our sexuality.

Much can be written about marriage, but this chapter will focus briefly only on the connection between sex and marriage and on the relationship between chastity and vocation.

## Sex and Marriage

We have said repeatedly that chastity is respecting sex so much that it is reserved for marriage. The key difference is that sex within marriage is a sacramental, an act that points to the sacrament of marriage. Vows said before God take on a spiritual significance, and the event becomes a sacrament—an encounter with God. The physical and spiritual reality is that two people become one. They are spiritually one because Jesus himself said that they would become one and should not be disjoined (Mt 19:5–6). They are physically one because two individuals are joined in marriage to become one new family.

A married couple has already given themselves fully to each other.

This separates sex in marriage from sex outside of marriage. A professed permanence exists in the marriage relationship. The spouses can give themselves fully—physically, intellectually, emotionally, and spiritually—without fear or need to hold back. They have done so in their marriage vows; this explains why the first act of sex is said to consummate, or complete, the marriage vows. Each act of sex then becomes a renewal of the marriage vows. Just as the vows promise permanent commitment, so does the act of sex. Outside of marriage, sex fails to renew a vow, because no vow exists.

Some people make a case that sex is acceptable if the couple is engaged. This is dangerous thinking. Yes, an engaged couple is pursuing marriage, but they are not yet married. I, Pete, have five close friends who have been engaged—one of them twice—and whose engagements were broken. Engagement is a sign that a permanent commitment may be coming, but it is not a replacement for the permanent commitment. Marriage is the only commitment that changes the context of sex.

Unfortunately, marriage in today's culture is not always seen as permanent commitment. For many, the view that marriage is a life-long commitment is simply a pie-in-the-sky ideal that cannot be reached. The Catholic Church, among others, continues to affirm that the permanent commitment of marriage is the norm and not the exception. In those circumstances in which a couple should separate or even divorce, the Church states that the spiritual union of the marriage may not be broken. This is why remarriage after a divorce is immoral in the eyes of the Church.

Does this sound unrealistic? It certainly is if one approaches marriage and sex from the perspective held by our popular culture. The problem, though, is not the ideal set forth by Jesus, but rather the low expectations of culture. It is much easier to say that faithfulness is impossible than it is to live faithfully. It is much easier to say that commitment is impossible than it is to be committed. It is much easier to say that self-giving love is impossible than it is to practice self-giving love. But many people ARE taking the hard road and ARE experiencing marriages filled with joy and happiness and excitement. These people have found a variety of different things that have helped each of them to experience a loving and fulfilling marriage. One of the common denominators leading to a great marriage is chastity.

## Chastity and Vocation

Chastity, as a part of God's loving plan, benefits everyone, regardless of one's current or future vocation. In God's plan, some of his children will give themselves in service to the Church as either a priest or a religious; some of his children will marry; and some will remain single. Chastity prepares and helps us for the vocation we follow.

Our vocation is a calling from God; it is a calling to live in a particular way. God calls all of us to grow in holiness, but our vocation is the particular path to holiness he desires for us. As such, any means by which we may grow in holiness will help to contribute to our vocation and prepare us for it. Chastity is one such means as it is a virtue of love, faithfulness, and self-giving.

Regardless of our vocation, there are important characteristics and qualities that help us to live our vocation better. Some of these, though not all, are as follows: developing good, healthy, fulfilling friendships with all sorts of people; increasing our ability to love others; becoming more Christlike; being faithful; ordering our desires properly; sacrificing our needs and wants for the good of another; acting unselfishly; and strengthening the skills necessary for a good marriage, or a good priesthood, a good religious life, or a healthy life as a single person. Chastity contributes to all of these.

Nothing is more damaging to a committed relationship than a lack of faithfulness to that commitment. The choice to live faithfully is a difficult one, especially in a sex-saturated culture that is filled with temptations. Chastity prepares us to be faithful in marriage because practicing chastity prior to marriage requires the same set of skills and abilities as practicing chastity in marriage.

To practice chastity, we must choose what is best for us—and possibly our future spouse—instead of immediate satisfaction. Those who practice chastity are developing the same skill of self-sacrifice that a good marriage (or priesthood) demands.

Living chastely in our relationships can help prepare us for our vocation. The freedom that chastity brings to dating relationships allows us to get to know ourselves well. It keeps us closer to God so that we can hear and respond to his call. It allows us to work on the skills and abilities that can positively impact our vocation: trust, communication, forgiveness, prayer and honesty.

Katie and Bill were the typical college couple. They started dating during their sophomore year; and their friends commented that Katie and Bill were so cute together, were the perfect couple, and seemed to be so right for each other. A few weeks into the relationship they began having sex; they were in a deeply committed relationship, and that is what each of them had always done in that type of relationship in the past. They were still dating during their junior year when several of their friends became engaged. Since they were pretty serious as well, they, too, became engaged. Like most engaged couples, they looked forward to their wedding and were married soon after they graduated. Within a year they were divorced. Neither one of them understood the commitment and both were unprepared to live it faithfully. Each of them failed to evaluate whether they should have married and whether they should have married each other. The sexual nature of their relationship did not help them. What became obvious to them after they married should have been evident beforehand.

Too many people are like Katie and Bill, they back into a vocation rather than pursuing it. When it comes time to live that vocation, they are horribly unprepared. Choosing chastity helps us to be ready for whatever vocation God calls us to.

# WHAT TO DO

· · · · · · · · · · · ·

## Chastity Sounds Nice, But Is It Practical and Realistic?

Here are some tried-and-true tips to help anyone live chastely, whether one is fourteen years old and desires to be pure for a lifetime or is an adult and starting over in chastity. These tips revolve around three key decisions: the decision to make a commitment to chastity, the decision to allow that commitment to change how one dates, and the decision to live in such a way as to make that commitment achievable.

## Make a Commitment to Chastity

*Make the commitment REAL.* Think of chastity as more than just a good idea; it's a virtue, so it holds no value unless you live it personally. People make the commitment in a variety of ways. Some sign a card; others wear a ring or write a letter to their future spouse. Whether or not you choose to do any of those, it is important to do something to make your commitment real.

*Know why you're committed to chastity.* If you choose chastity, at least one person will ask why you have done this. The answers vary for every individual, but be prepared to offer more than "My Church and my parents tell me to." That argument won't last long and most likely won't help you stand firm for a lifetime. The more you know about chastity, the deeper it can penetrate your heart and life. Many resources are available for learning more about chastity (see Appendix A, page 157).

*Be vocal about your decision.* You don't need to tell the world, but don't be ashamed to let others know of your decision. If you are dating someone, that person needs to know your views up front. Nothing is more frustrating to a date than being misled.

*Find an accountability partner or mentor.* Ask a friend or mentor to help keep you accountable to your decision. Give your accountability partner permission to ask tough questions after dates and as a relationship progresses. You can choose a parent, youth minister, teacher, priest, or anyone else who truly wants the best for you, is grounded in faith, and is a role model of chastity.

## Date Differently

*Leave unhealthy relationships.* If you realize that a relationship is unchaste or unhealthy in any other way, pray for guidance and courage and walk away. Staying in a bad relationship causes severe damage to future relationships.

*Focus on friendships.* During the teen and young adult years, the ability to make and keep healthy friendships with members of the complementary sex will help you much more in future meaningful relationships than will the typical pattern of "dating around." Focus on friendship first, before dating someone; this ensures that the relationship is built on more than physical attraction. Some of the best relationships start with incredible friendships.

*Be selective about your friends and those you date.* Many people choose chastity and then wonder why their values disappear so quickly in high school or college. If this is your experience, ask yourself, "Who are my friends? Do they value chastity?" It may be very difficult to find friends who practice chastity, but it is essential to do so. Before going out with someone, be sure he or she has embraced chastity as well. If someone abstains only because you force him or her, be very careful. When the desire for chastity is held more strongly by one rather than by both persons, the relationship tends to become filled with unhealthy pressure and frustration. This doesn't mean that all of your friends must live chastely or they can't be your friends. Rather, it will be difficult for you to live your commitment to chastity if most of your friends have chosen different values.

> After experiencing many heartbreaking relationships, Julie made a strong commitment to chastity at the age of seventeen. She soon met and began to date a chaste Christian guy, and she loved the peace and fulfillment they enjoyed in their relationship. When they broke up, she began hanging out with a new group of friends. Although she tried to tell these individuals that chastity is an incredible virtue for dating, these new friends didn't listen. They challenged her values often and even lightly teased the "prude." Although Julie thought she was strong in her commitment to chastity, she slowly started to think that maybe it was an unrealistic idea; maybe something was wrong with her. Then, when she dated one of these new friends, things progressed quickly. She felt weak and unable to stand up for herself and her values. She became pregnant at the age of twenty-two; the father of her child did not even love her.

*Set physical limits/boundaries with each person you date.* Different people have different ideas about sex. When you begin to date someone, learn about his or her sexual values. Openly discuss your hopes for purity in a physical relationship.[41] You need to determine how far you will go physically and what you will do if you get close to the limit. When a couple has a plan of action which holds each other accountable, they can lessen the tension in the physical relationship.

*Plan dates to avoid surprises and long periods of time alone.* It will be much easier to remain pure in a relationship and keep your physical boundaries if you avoid places and situations of temptation.

Include family members or friends as part of your fun. If you desire alone time with your boyfriend or girlfriend, go to a public place where you can share privately but without the temptation to do things physically. As the relationship develops, you will spend more time alone with each other, but be aware of how tempting situations can become.

## Live Differently

*Find strength in prayer and sacraments.* Living chastely is tough, and few, if any, of us can do it on our own. Fortunately, God's grace is abundant and more than adequate to help us. Prayer, especially daily prayer, can orient your heart and mind to God. When your heart and mind are in union with God, you will be able to live chastely. Pray before every date. Pray for your future spouse.

The sacraments, especially Eucharist and reconciliation, are two of our biggest allies in living a chaste life. Eucharist gives us the grace and strength to be like Christ in all ways, especially in purity. Reconciliation restores and strengthens our relationship with God and restores our resolve to be faithful. Reconciliation also removes the guilt and shame often associated with sexual sins. Whenever you fail in your attempts at chastity, reconciliation can help you to start over.

*Stay sober.* Drinking has an impact on our sexual choices. Our values often get thrown to the wind because drugs and alcohol blur our sense of reality. Also, when we are sober, our physical displays of affection are much more complimentary to others than when we are drunk.

Kathy says, "Lou and I were friends for years. But we both had too much to drink that night. Our intention was that a bunch of friends would join us for a swim. Instead, with just the two of us in the pool, barely clothed and intoxicated, one thing quickly led to

another. We were both shocked at how easily the commitment
to chastity disappeared after some drinks and being in an un-
usual situation."

*Keep a pure mind.* As mentioned previously, what goes into our brains through TV, movies, and music will come out in some way. Avoid sexually explicit references or displays so that you can keep your mind always focused on honoring sex and members of the complementary sex. Reading Scripture frequently will help you to stay focused on real love. When you are in a romantic mood, read the Old Testament's Song of Solomon to keep your thoughts focused on God's plan for your sexuality.

*Think of your future spouse at tempting moments.* Always re-member that everything you do now will affect your future marriage or vocation in both positive and negative ways. In living chastely, the good things you do today and the good decisions you make today are strengthening your future marriage.

## How Can Women Live Chastely?

The previous chapter presented some general principles for living and growing in the virtue of chastity. Each of those principles is relevant for both men and women. However, God has made us with healthy differences, and often our struggles and temptations in living chastely are different. With that in mind, we offer some additional suggestions that are targeted directly toward teenage and young adult women who are interested in being chaste. (Teenage and young adult men will find suggestions in the following chapter.) The following advice is from Heather.

## Stay Emotionally Strong, Not Crushed or Cold

Women, we are made emotionally strong. God gave us this gift. Even when we are very young we are usually much more in touch with and able to articulate our emotions than guys. Guys are different. They may experience deep emotions without the ability to understand what's happening as clearly or to describe it. Due to this difference between men and women, it's important that we don't hand over all of our emotions too early in our relationships with them. Guys often don't know how to deal with the intensity of our hearts.

Some of my dearest friends gave their hearts away early and completely in relationships, and only tears and much pain remained when those relationships ended. To stay emotionally healthy and ready to trust and love the right guy, guard and treasure the beauty of the gift you have been given. If you or a woman you know has become

138

emotionally cold and heartless as a result of the pain of bad relationships, pray for restoration. It is unnatural for women to be emotionally vulnerable and then to be stomped on. Becoming vulnerable again when married will be difficult, but with God's grace it can be done.

## Find and Cling to Good Guys of All Ages

Most of what we women learn about men is learned from our fathers. How your dad has treated you strongly determines how you will respond to guys later in life. If your father has showered love, attention, and affection on you, you are less likely to turn to guys to fill the void. If not, having good male mentors and friends can help make up for a father's lack of love. This will enhance your self-esteem, even if you've been blessed by your father's affection. Male friends and mentors who have no desire to use you or look at you with anything other than love can remind you, when you're tempted to believe otherwise, that good guys do exist.

## Build Self-Esteem From Girlfriends

The majority of your self-esteem boosters should come from members of the same sex. Before you marry, especially while you are still in your teens, you should relish the time you have simply to be a young woman. Soak yourself in positive female friendships. You need women around you who love, respect, and accept you for who you are, including bad hair, "pathetic" clothes, and not knowing what to say. If you limit your relationships to guys whom you might date, you run the risk of having little stability; guys are apt to come and go. Great girlfriends stick around and will boost your self-esteem and femininity in ways that guys never can.

## Help Girlfriends and Women in General

*Bug your friends when they're dating.* Ask your girlfriends, "Does your date respect you?" You can help your friends by gently reminding them that they deserve respect and honor and shouldn't settle for anything less. Although they may be annoyed at the time, they should appreciate your concern and reminders later.

*Rebel Against the Media.* Women today are constantly bombarded with images of how they should look—large breasts, flawless face, flat stomach, and shapely legs. Every aspect of feminine beauty is defined by media standards. If you want to help yourself, your friends, and other women discover the beauty that lies beneath the surface, rebel against the media. Focus on personality, humor, intelligence, and spirit, things often overlooked in the media. Refuse to watch television programs that portray women as merely objects for male enjoyment.

## Help Men by Raising Standards

Sometimes guys haven't learned how to treat women. Maybe their parents didn't model true respect or their previous girlfriends didn't require respect. Therefore, it is important to help guys learn what it means to respect a woman and how much women value a man of true honor. I dated a guy once who didn't respect me well. However, I kept strong, but we eventually stopped seeing each other. Although I'm not sure what's going on in his life now, I am willing to bet that our relationship changed his mind about the value of respect. Maybe he's been treating his new girlfriends a little nicer because of me.

Ladies, most men will respect us if we expect and require them to do so. If we don't care about how we are treated, men who want to take advantage of women will find us and treat us disrespectfully. If we demand respect, however, they have no other option—respect us or leave. The good news is that not all of them leave.

My freshman roommate in college, Amy, was cute, friendly, and had incredibly high standards. Two things specifically shocked me about her practice of chastity—she wouldn't allow her boyfriend to hold her in a certain way, and she was terribly disgusted by a sexual scene in a movie that we watched early in the year. I thought she was just a bit overboard. However, the boys kept calling for her, and she dated frequently. She was pretty, but not a super-model. Regardless, guys saw her beauty within, loved being with her, and treated her like gold. I benefitted too; I didn't mind great guys hanging out in my room! Amy taught guys, as well as her roommate, about true respect.

## Help Guys View Us As People, Not Objects

Women, we can't begin to understand how easy it is for a guy to be stimulated just by what he sees—men are extremely visual! For some guys, just seeing parts of a woman revealed—a little cleavage or belly button or a bare back—gets them thinking about what they would do with such a body. They literally use and discard women in their minds. We can help men see our eyes, smiles, and personalities when we cover what most distracts men. Dressing modestly really helps guys to remain pure and to view women as whole people. We need to show them that our interior beauty is more important than the beauty they see on the outside. Men really are intrigued by a woman who doesn't bare everything. She exudes mystery; she embodies a secret that must be honored and respected.

> Sara made a decision for chastity in junior high. As she grew older, she dressed modestly. Though she had a good figure, she didn't accentuate it with tight, low-cut, revealing clothes. She maintained her modesty throughout her dating relationships and even through her engagement. On her wedding night, when

- she took off her wedding dress, the look of genuine surprise
- and amazement on her husband's face was a source of great
- joy for her. Modesty not only helped Sara to live chastely, it also
- added to her honeymoon experience.

## Look to the Model of Feminine Strength and Beauty

When we struggle with living chastely as women, we need to talk to our moms. Yes, our earthly mothers can be quite helpful, but our mother in heaven, Mary, is constantly available to listen to us and extremely faithful in praying for us when we seek her assistance. We can pray a rosary and seek Mary's help in keeping our commitment to chastity. I always say a Hail Mary before going on a date and ask her to pray for both of us. Mary is a role model of purity, chastity, and unfailing commitment to God's call.

I encourage you to be bold about your purity and chastity. Many lives can be affected if you stand up for what is truly beautiful, respectful, and loving.

• • •

Finally, this chapter would not be complete without some advice from Pete to young women who are seeking to live chastely. From a male point of view, these are some suggestions.

## Attract What You Want—Use Good Bait to Find Good Guys

Most women I know do not desire to be used and abused by men. However, so many of my friends have often said, "Why am I a jerk-magnet?" Have you ever gone fishing? If you want to catch a trout, you use different bait than you use to try to catch bass. Please consider the "bait" you are using to attract men. If you want a boyfriend who is interested in your body, wear immodest and provocative clothing and carry yourself seductively. If, however, you want a boyfriend who is interested in you, dress modestly and carry yourself respectfully. Sure, you may not catch the eye of every guy at the party, but the guys you do attract will truly be more interested in you as a person. Likewise, if you want a guy who values his relationship with God, don't spend a lot of time at parties with alcohol and drugs. You are more likely to meet him at a youth group meeting or at Sunday Mass.

## Be Honest and Upfront

Let the guys you meet know that your expectations are different. This is why it helps to become friends first and date second. During the course of getting to know you as a friend, guys will be able to find out that you are looking for a relationship that is chaste. To be honest, letting guys know that you are not interested in a sexual relationship can run off those guys looking for sex in a relationship. This can be discouraging, but what you will be left with are men who want to honor and respect you.

## Don't Sell Out

This can be the hardest task of all. When it seems as though everyone else has a boyfriend, any boyfriend can seem preferable to no boyfriend. Please do not buy into the lie that says you have to be dating to be normal or complete. It can be hard to be selective; but be selective for your own good. You are quite selective in other areas of your life, such as your physical health and the foods you eat; be even more selective when it comes to relational and emotional health. A lot of harm can come from being in the wrong relationship or in an unhealthy one. On the other hand, much good can come from being patient and selective in terms of whom you date.

## How Can Men Live Chastely?

In a previous chapter (page 138), we discussed some general principles for how to live out and grow in the virtue of chastity. Each of those principles is relevant for both men and women. However, in this chapter, we offer some additional suggestions that are targeted directly toward teenage and young-adult men who are interested in being chaste. God has made us with healthy differences, and often our struggles and temptations in living chastely are different. With that in mind, we offer this advice from Pete.

### Know Yourself

Knowing yourself will help you practice chastity. A large part of living chastely is avoiding temptation. Some temptations are obvious, for example, pornography; others are not. Successfully avoiding temptation requires us to know what temptations are most difficult for us to overcome and in which areas of sexuality we are the weakest. Knowing ourselves takes time and effort. Prayerful reflection is an important part of growing in self-knowledge. Taking time to learn from our experiences, though challenging at times, is also helpful.

### Control Your Thought Life

For most men, the greatest sexual temptations begin in our minds. When the images and ideas that dominate our thoughts are unhealthy, we find it difficult to act in healthy ways. How we think about women affects how we relate with them, how we treat them, and how well we love them. It may seem like part of our nature to think sexually about women, to undress them in our minds, or even to fantasize about being physically intimate with them; but God calls us to a higher standard. He calls us to think about sex in terms of a husband and wife uniting themselves together in marriage.

I will share five quick things that I and some male friends of mine have found helpful in the midst of our sex-saturated culture.

*First, watch what you watch.* Excessive intake of sexual images from television and movies and any intake of pornography can have drastic and negative affects on our thoughts. These effects can linger long after the image is removed.

*Second, practice the three-second rule.* In just three seconds, you can get a good idea of a woman's beauty and appreciate that beauty. Looking at a woman longer than three seconds often causes the male mind to go beyond her beauty into unhealthy areas. For some, the three-second rule should be replaced with the three-millisecond rule. As I said, knowing yourself is important.

*Third, make good eye contact.* When looking at and talking to women, consider where your eyes are focused. If you are staring at her chest, chances are your thoughts aren't about how much you appreciate her intellect and her personality.

*Fourth, be grateful.* When tempted by your thoughts, say a prayer of gratitude. Thank God that you are a man. Thank God for your gift of sexuality. Temptation to sin is temptation to turn away from God. A spirit of gratitude towards God brings us closer to him.

*Finally, pray.* Nothing is more helpful than turning our thoughts and minds to God in prayer. In prayer we can find healing for past sexual sins that haunt us and affect our thought life. In prayer we can turn over to God all of our temptations. In prayer we can receive the grace to think about our sexuality in God-like ways. In prayer we receive the strength to live purity fully—in body and mind.

## Honor and Respect Women

One of the great contributions of psychological research is an understanding that human beings can be trained. Regardless of what rut or negative processes we are stuck in, we can condition ourselves to act and think in different, more positive ways. In terms of chastity, our culture has frequently conditioned us to respond sexually. This kind of conditioning can often be difficult to overcome.

The good news, at least where chastity is concerned, is that we can learn to respect and honor women by doing things that respect and honor them. As we begin to act in new, positive ways, our old negative attitudes and thoughts may resurface. But as we continue to do positive things, our brains eventually catch on, and we become conditioned toward honoring and respecting women. The more we do it, the easier it becomes until eventually our respect for women becomes natural in our relationships.

This book is full of ways to honor and respect women, but it is good to mention a few here. Treat women as people, not objects. Let them know you are concerned about their well-being. Act on that concern. Be interested in their thoughts and feelings. Spend time getting to know who they are on the inside. Make them feel special by the way you treat them. Make an effort to get to know and become friends with their friends and even their families. Be interested and concerned about women you don't want to date, not simply those that you do. Serve them; do things for them that you don't have to do but that you want to do for them. Give up something important to you to do something important for them. In all ways, treat them the way you would want your father to treat your mother or your brother-in-law to treat your sister. Doing these things does not guarantee that all women will love you, but you will find few women who prefer to be treated any other way by a man.

## Male Accountability

One of the biggest helps for me and a number of men I know is accountability. I meet with other men regularly, and we share how we are doing in the area of chastity; this helps us stay accountable to the goals of living chastely. We support one another when we do well and when we fall. We pray together when one of us is struggling and in need. More than once, a friend has said that knowing he would have to admit failure to the group helped him to think twice about sinning. This type of accountability can be very helpful in our attempts to live chastely.

## Use Other Venues for Sexual Energy

Just about every guy knows that the sexual drive is one of our strongest. As we discussed in previous chapters, giving in to that drive increases rather than decreases its strength. However, it is possible to take sexual energy and reroute it into other activities. Exercise is perhaps the easiest diversion. Regular physical exercise can be a release of sexual tension and energy; the energy is spent without increasing sexual desire. Another venue is service, especially manual labor. Our sexual drive often tries to get us to focus on ourselves and our own sexual needs. Service, by its nature, forces us to focus on other people and their needs. Taking that energy and using it for such positive results is very helpful.

## Avoid Compromising Positions

Part of knowing ourselves is knowing what situations tempt us. Though we have mentioned this in the chapter on general advice, some concerns are particular to men. By nature, men tend to be more visually stimulated than women, and some circumstances are more sexually arousing for men than they might be for women.

Also, men tend to be the sexual initiator. This means that many times it is the man who seeks to control the situation. Therefore, we men have a responsibility to avoid circumstances that compromise chastity. If I know that lying together on the couch and kissing passionately is unhealthy for me in terms of my chastity, then I have an obligation to avoid doing this. But I also have a responsibility to avoid sitting on the couch and initiating passionate kissing that leads me to want to lie down together on the couch.

## Get to Know Women Before You Date Them

In our culture, the pressures to date seem overwhelming. I see this in middle-school students who are gearing up for a mixer and in high-school students preparing for their weekend activities. The trend seems to be to get to know someone through dating. While it is true that you should grow in your knowledge and understanding of who your girlfriend is while you are dating her, it is better to get to know her before you start dating her. Maybe I'm too countercultural, but my wife was only the fourth woman that I dated. Sure, I went out and did things with a number of other women, sometimes one-on-one, but these were always occasions to hang out as friends.

If getting to know someone well takes place after the decision to date is made, on what is that decision based? If it is simply physical attraction, then the relationship is starting off on a shallow basis. If, however, the relationship emerges out of an existing friendship, then the relationship already has some depth and a healthier basis for growth.

So what does this have to do with chastity? A relationship in which the couple can spend a lot of time together relating and having fun without getting physical has a better chance at being chaste. It also means you have something to build upon relationally. Otherwise, the relationship almost always attempts to grow physically—a sure and certain danger for living chastely.

Many ways exist for getting to know women before dating them. Going out with people in groups is the best way to get to know people. Having meaningful conversations and seeking to get to know women is also helpful. Planning more relational dating activities, such as going out to dinner or hanging out at a park, can help to build friendships. Even going out one on one, just as friends, is a good way to get to know someone else. Ultimately, seeking to be friends first can help avoid unhealthy relationships and make it easier, in relationships, to be chaste.

• • •

As Pete did in the previous chapter, Heather now adds some suggestions on chastity for young men from a female point of view. A major obstacle for many men, however, is women. Some of the following tips focus on how you can help women. These tips will keep you healthy and strong as well.

## Set Your Own Sexual Values

As a woman, the most uncomfortable romantic relationships I've experienced are with guys who force the girl to set all the physical boundaries with the attitude that "I'll do whatever she lets me do." It's not fun for me—or for most other girls either—constantly to be a "chastity guard" when I'm trying to enjoy an evening with a guy. If a girl becomes offended because you're not pushing her physically, tell her that you want to take things slow because you care about her. If she doesn't respect how you honor her or if she pushes you about your values, don't waste your time with her.

## Guard the Hearts of Women

Women are typically more in touch with their emotions and are often able to articulate and give them away very early in relationships.

Please help women by letting them know if their emotions are scaring you. Josh wasn't ready for a relationship and he told me that as soon as it became clear that we were attracted to each other. He sensed that we had feelings for each other, and he didn't want to lead me on. I was thankful that he told me that before I fell for him. It saved my heart from being crushed. Also, if you're not feeling intense emotions for a girl, please don't use her emotions to your advantage.

## Help Women Focus on Their Inner Beauty

Eating disorders, excessive tanning, hours upon hours on the treadmill, or not stepping outside without a pound of makeup describes many women I've met. Most guys I know are not very intrigued by such ladies, and you can do much to help them and all women by the way you treat them.

Here is an example of what not to do:

> Brian and I were good friends in college—we would talk for hours at a time. On several occasions when I was on campus early in the morning—for ballet class or a jog—before my shower, Brian wouldn't acknowledge me when he saw me, especially when his friends were around. But two days later, when I was dressed up at a party, he greeted me with a big smile and hug.

And here is an example of what to do to help women:

> Will had only seen me dressed up and wearing makeup. When a group of friends went out one night, I happened not to be wearing makeup and my hair was a mess; I hadn't planned to go out. Will paid me as much attention that night as he did on the earlier

occasions. I actually think he paid more attention because he knew I wasn't out to impress him. The way he treated me gave me the freedom to be myself and not to worry about how I looked around him or other guys.

You can help all women, not just those you know, by your actions. Women notice if guys are constantly checking out women in public, "wowing" at the sexy girl on TV, or viewing porn or sexy pictures of women. We desire to impress guys; we want to be valuable to you. If we learn that you highly value toned legs, big breasts, and so forth, then we'll feel less valuable to you if we don't have these attributes. Many women will do everything—even unhealthy things—so they can look that way for you.

You can do several things to counter women's desire to be physically perfect. First, please don't stare at the shallow exhibits of women's bodies—on television, in magazines, in public. This helps your thought life as well as our self-esteem. Second, compliment a woman when she's not wearing the sexiest of outfits but just catches your attention. Finally, compliment a woman on her smile, eyes—or better yet—the things you love about her personality. You have no idea how much power you have to impact women.

# ZERO REGRETS

## The Decision Is Yours

After hearing our "case" for chastity, you have the opportunity to give the final verdict. Let us leave you with a few final thoughts.

## Trusting Reality

In 1976, during the Summer Olympics in Montreal, Japanese gymnast Shun Fujimoto accomplished a truly remarkable feat. During the floor exercise, he broke his kneecap. His team needed his scores to compete for a gold medal, so he mounted the rings and performed his entire routine, all the while knowing that at the end he would have to dismount. His dismount would take him fifteen to twenty feet into the air, and if he wanted to score well, he would have to stick the landing. As Fujimoto was in the air, he knew that to land on both feet would cause excruciating pain; how much he didn't know.

This example provides an analogy to engaging in sex outside of marriage. The reality is that there will be consequences, some more painful or more damaging than others; and we do not know precisely what they will be. On the contrary, when we choose chastity, we know what the consequences will be—greater freedom, truly loving relationships, increased virtue and holiness in our lives, a lifestyle without regrets, and a sexual union in marriage which we can look forward to experiencing in deep and passionate ways.

You have read the stories of a number of people whom we know; you have read about their experiences with sex and chastity. We could have chosen countless more to share with you. If there is one common denominator, though, it is that almost everyone who has chosen to have sex outside of marriage expresses some degree of regret about those decisions. Everyone who has chosen chastity has done so without regret.

> In seventh grade, Kalen first learned about chastity. Though she wasn't very interested in boys at the time, the message given by real people with real stories made sense. So she signed a chastity commitment card. Now, as a gorgeous ivy-league student, Kalen still carries her card with her and wears a ring proclaiming her chastity. She speaks to young people on the topic. "I'm just thankful that I made a commitment to chastity so young. I've avoided all the baggage, heartache, and problems my friends continue to endure from sexual relationships. The decision for chastity has brought great guys into my life and provided me the freedom to experience incredible opportunities—there's never a dull moment in my life and I wouldn't have it any other way."

## Trusting God's Grace

The truth is that chastity is not the easiest of choices, though it is the best. God never promised us an easy life; in the Bible, Jesus tells his followers to take up the cross and follow him. Sometimes, living chastely is difficult and feels like a heavy cross to bear. The consequences, though, of doing what God desires for us are never bad for us. They may be difficult or challenging or even seem impossible without God's grace, but they are never bad for us.

We can take comfort in knowing that we do not need to bear this cross by ourselves. God is a tremendous source of grace for us as we struggle to live as he desires; and God freely offers that grace to us. Hundreds of thousands of teenagers and young adults are embracing chastity and finding comfort and support in one another. We may travel a rocky road, but we do not travel alone.

> Jay was seriously dating Connie while they were in college. Though they chose not to have sex, they were not living chastely. At a young adult conference one summer, Jay felt God calling him to greater chastity. He knew that it would probably mean ending the relationship, something that was going to be difficult for him. Jay prayed for God's grace to do the right thing. As a result, he was able to break off his relationship with Connie and recommit himself to living chastely in his future relationships.

## Trusting God's Plan

Imagine that a large bowl of cereal has been placed before you, and you are hungry for breakfast. Next to the bowl are a butcher knife, a fork, and a spoon, and you are free to use any of these utensils for eating the cereal. Which one would you choose? That should be a "duh!" answer. If you use the butcher knife, you most likely won't get much cereal and will probably cut yourself. If you use the fork, you will get some cereal but little milk, and the experience will be less than it should be. However, if you choose the spoon, you will be able to enjoy the bowl of cereal completely.

Our attempts to find real love and true freedom by dating and building relationships can be likened to eating this bowl of cereal. Living according to the unchaste norms of popular culture is like trying to eat cereal with a knife. Although it seems dangerous and exciting, you gain so little of what you need and could get seriously hurt. Merely abstaining from intercourse is like eating the cereal with a fork. We get more nutrients—more love and respect—but never the complete fulfillment that we most desire. However, when we completely trust God and choose his plan of chastity, it is like eating the bowl of cereal with the spoon. We not only gain real love and true freedom, but also an incredible relationship with God and great sex if called to marriage.

As a popular eighth-grader, with skater clothes and a good heart, Joe often attracted the ladies. One in particular wanted Joe's attention. Leslie showed up at Joe's house one day, when his parent's weren't home. Joe knew she had been struggling with family issues, so he was prepared to listen and advise her. Looking for intimacy the best way she knew how, Leslie offered to give Joe oral sex. Even though Joe thought Leslie was cute, he said, "No." She asked, "Why not?" (Some of his friends asked the same question.) Joe explained his commitment to chastity, but more importantly his desire to respect her, and not to take advantage of her. Joe's confidence soared afterwards because he realized that with God's help, he could live chastely. Joe still considers his chaste behavior a "chick-magnet" because he knows women most desire true respect. He has the courage to honor them even when they don't respect themselves. When thinking back on Leslie's offer, he has no regrets and claims, "I saved her from herself."

Monica and her boyfriend had been sexually active for a while before Monica went on her senior retreat. During one of the talks, she heard about chastity. She realized that she and her boyfriend were missing out on the love and freedom the speaker described in her relationships. Monica desired chastity, but had no idea how her boyfriend would respond. He really enjoyed having sex. But she took two chastity commitment cards with her and went to her boyfriend's house. She told him about chastity that afternoon.

She concluded by saying, "So, I think we should stop having sex." And, guess what her boyfriend said? He said, "All right." He loved her and the relationship more than the sex.

Jeremy was fourteen when he made a decision for chastity. He signed a chastity commitment card and put it in his wallet. He didn't know who or if he'd ever marry, but he wanted to respect and honor women and thought trusting God might be worth it in the end. At the age of twenty-six, he was still committed to chastity—even in the face of ridicule from peers for "waiting so long." Then he fell in love with the woman of his dreams. They dated for months and he knew she was the one. In considering how to propose marriage, he thought of all the great gifts he might give her. Then he decided. One Sunday evening, he got down on one knee, took out a diamond ring and asked, "Will you marry me?" She said, "Yes." Then, still down on one knee, he pulled out of his wallet the chastity commitment card he'd signed years ago and said, "I've waited my whole life for you." Her heart melted immediately. There was no better gift he could have given her than that. He also claims their honeymoon was quite an adventure.

It is our hope and prayer for you that you will see clearly the beauty of God's plan for your sexuality. We desire for you to choose the virtue of chastity as the best expression of the gift of sex God has given to you. A lifestyle with joy and without regret awaits you. With confidence, take hold of everything God desires for you and has made available to you. Choose chastity.

# APPENDIX A
. . . . . . . . . . .

## Where Else Can I Turn?

As with any topic, no one book can give you everything definitively. While we have tried to cover a full range of topics when it comes to teenagers and sexuality, we certainly haven't touched on everything. The following lists of resources are to be a guide for further study and reading on chastity. The Appendix itself is certainly not a complete list of resources, but we have tried to include those things that we know are good and either ourselves or others we know have found to be helpful.

## Church Teaching

*The Catechism of the Catholic Church.* The latest edition, released in 1994 and revised in 1997, is the most comprehensive teaching of the Catholic faith since the Second Vatican Council. It is a great starting point for understanding any of the teachings of the Catholic Church. It is available online at several sources, but the site for the U.S. Conference of Catholic Bishops <www.usccb.org/catechism/text /index.htm> is a good place to start. Please keep in mind that as good of a resource as the *Catechism* is, it was not written with teenagers and young adults as target audiences. That doesn't mean that young people aren't capable of reading and understanding what the *Catechism* says. Rather, it means that sometimes the *Catechism* can raise as many questions as it answers. Please find someone you can speak to about questions that may come up—a parish priest, for example.

## Statements of the United States Bishops on Marriage and Sexuality

These documents may be found in their entirety at <www.usccb.org>. An alternative way to locate a particular text is to put its title in a search engine. They are listed chronologically and, in some cases, also listed alphabetically.

*Living the Gospel of Life: A Challenge to American Catholics.* A statement by the Catholic Bishops of the United States. November 18, 1988.

*A Matter of the Heart.* A Statement of the United States Conference of Catholic Bishops on the Thirtieth Anniversary of *Roe v. Wade.* November 12, 2002.

## Papal Encyclicals and Apostolic Letters and Exhortations on Marriage and Sexuality

All of the encyclicals and other documents that follow are available on the Internet, the Vatican's own Web site; <www.vatican.va> has them along with related reading material. They are listed alphabetically.

*Evangelium Vitae* (The Gospel of Life), Pope John Paul II, March 25, 1995.

*Familiaris Consortio* (On the Role of the Christian Family in the Modern World), Pope John Paul II, November 22, 1981 (Apostolic Exhortation).

*Humanae Vitae* (On the Regulation of Birth), Pope Paul VI, July 25, 1968.

*Mulieris Dignitatem* (Letter on the Dignity and Vocation of Women), Pope John Paul II, June 29, 1995 (Apostolic Letter).

*Redemptionis Donum* (To Men and Women Religious on Their Consecration in the Light of the Mystery of Redemption), Pope John Paul II, March 25, 1984 (Apostolic Exhortation).

*Sacerdotalis Caelibatus* (On the Celibacy of the Priest), Pope Paul VI, June 24, 1967.

*Veritatis Splendor* (The Splendor of Truth—Regarding Certain Fundamental Question of the Church's Moral Teaching), Pope John Paul II, August 6, 1993.

## Books for Teens and Young Adults

The following represent three of the best Catholic books on the subject of chastity.

Bonacci, Mary Beth. *Real Love: Answers to Your Questions on Dating, Marriage and the Real Meaning of Sex*. San Francisco: Ignatius Press, 1996.

Evert, Jason. *If You Really Loved Me: 101 Questions on Dating, Relationships, and Sexual Purity*. Ann Arbor, Mich.: Servant Publications, 2003.

West, Christopher. *Good News About Sex and Marriage: Answers to Your Honest Questions About Catholic Teaching*. Ann Arbor, Mich.: Servant Publications, 2000.

The following books are recommended for teens and young adults. They are listed alphabetically by author.

Arterburn, Stephen, Fred Stoeker, and Mike Yorkey. *Every Young Man's Battle: Strategies for Victory in the Real World of Sexual Temptation*. Colorado Springs, Col.: Waterbrook Press, 2002.

Elliot, Elisabeth. *Passion and Purity: Learning to Bring Your Love Life Under Christ's Control*. Grand Rapids, Mich.: Fleming H. Revell Co., 2002.

Harris, Joshua. *Boy Meets Girl: Say Hello to Courtship*. Portland, Ore.: Multnomah Publishers, 2000.

_____. *I Kissed Dating Goodbye: A New Attitude Toward Relationships and Romance*. Portland, Ore.: Multnomah Publishers, 1997.

John Paul II. *The Meaning of Vocation*. Princeton, N.J.: Scepter Publications, 1998.

Johnson, Greg. *258 Great Dates While You Wait*. Nashville, Tenn.: Broadman & Holman, 1995.

Kiser Keith and Tami Kiser. *The Incredible Gift: The Truth About Love and Sex*. Huntington, Ind.: Our Sunday Visitor, 1996.

Likona, Tom and Judy Lickona, et. al. *Sex, Love & You: Making the Right Decisions*. Notre Dame, Ind.: Ave Maria Press, 2003.

Ludy, Eric and Leslie Ludy. *When God Writes Your Love Story*. Sisters, Ore.: Loyal Publishing, 1999.

## Books for Mature Teens, Adults, and Parents.

Evert, Jason and Ellen Marie. "Parents of Teens: What You Need to Know." Vision Video, Color, NTSC format, 2002. To order, call 1-800-858-3040 or go to www. Heritagehouse76.com.

Finn, Thomas and Donna Finn. *Intimate Bedfellows: Love, Sex, and the Catholic Church*. Boston: St. Paul Books & Media, 1993.

Groeschel, Benedict J. *Courage to Be Chaste*. Mahwah, N.J.: Paulist Press, 1988.

Hogan, Richard M. and John Levoir. *Covenant of Love: Pope John Paul II on Sexuality, Marriage, and Family in the Modern World*. San Francisco: Ignatius Press, 1992.

McDowell, Josh and Dick Day. *Why Wait? What You Need to Know About the Teen Sexuality Crisis*. Nashville, Tenn.: Thomas Nelson, 1994.

Raunikar, Dan. *Choosing God's Best*. Portland, Ore.: Multnomah, 2000.

Shalit, Wendy. *A Return to Modesty: Discovering the Lost Virtue.* Riverside, N.J.: Simon & Schuster (Touchstone Books), 2000.

West, Christopher. *Theology of the Body Explained: A Commentary on John Paul II's "Gospel of the Body."* Boston: Pauline Books & Media, 2003.

Wojtyla, Karol (Pope John Paul II). *Love and Responsibility.* San Francisco: Ignatius Press, 1994.

## Web Sites

The REAP Team <http://www.reapteam.org>. The Chastity Challenge portion includes testimonies from teens, celebrities, tips for living chastity, and answers to many related questions.

Real Love Productions <ttp://www.reallove.net> includes articles by Mary Beth Bonacci for teens and young adults.

LIFE TEEN <http://lifeteen.org> answers many teen questions on sex and chastity throughout the site.

Love Matters <http://www.lovematters.com> is an excellent Christian source on dating, sex, and love. Contains articles on chastity, secondary virginity, STDs, finding true love, and gives guidelines for answering the question, "Is it true love?"

Catholic Answers <http://www.catholic.com/chastity> gives information on chastity seminars and answers questions about practicing chastity.

Pro-Life America <http://www.prolife.com> gives information on learning how to survive in today's sex culture and important tips on dating, sex, love, and life, such as "Ten Dangers of Sex Too Soon," "A Couple's First Kiss," and "How to Say 'No.'" Also includes pro-life information.

It's Great to Wait <http://www.greattowait.com> shows why the best choice is abstinence until marriage.

Not Me, Not Now <http://www.notmenotnow.org> offers information to reinforce the abstinence message at school, at home, and in your community.

Love Smarts <http://www.lovesmarts.org> is for college students who want to have intelligent relationships. Also offers books, a teen newsletter, CD-ROM Powerpoint presentations, and videos.

*Christianity Today* <http://www.christianitytoday.com/teens>, through its offshoot aimed at college students (*Campus Life*), answers many questions about sex and dating, building good relationships, and even includes some humor.

The Medical Institute for Sexual Health <http:// www.medinstitute.org> identifies, evaluates, and communicates credible scientific data in an understandable way in order to promote healthy and godly sexual decisions. Includes information on STDs.

Free To Be Me <http://www.freetobeme.com> is sponsored by New Direction for Life Ministries, an organization which works with men and women who choose to leave homosexuality. It offers resources for those who work with youth and also discusses homosexuality issues.

 Courage <http://couragerc.net> is an apostolate of the Catholic Church and ministers to those with same-sex attractions and their loved ones. It offers a special section on homosexuality issues for youth.

National Association for Research and Therapy of Homosexuality (NARTH) <http://www.narth.com> is an organization whose primary goal is to make effective psychological therapy available to all homosexual men and women who seek change.

National Office of Post Abortion Reconciliation and Healing <http://www.noparh.org> offers links to support groups, related Web sites, and recommended books.

Pure Intimacy <http://www.pureintimacy.org> addresses online sexual temptation and offering resources that may help to fight the temptations of online pornography.

Desert Stream Ministries <http://www.desertstream.org> ministers the life of Jesus to the sexually and relationally broken. It offers resources, programs, testimonies, conferences, and newsletters .

The Gift Foundation <http://www.giftfoundation.org> provides excellent Catholic sexuality educational resources, featuring John Paul II's *Theology of the Body.*

Couple to Couple League <http://www.ccli.org> is a resource for those wanting to learn more about Natural Family Planning.

One More Soul <http://www.omsoul.com> is dedicated to spreading the truth about the blessings of children and the harm of contraception. It offers a wide variety of education resources, including tapes, videos, and books, pro-life articles, and links.

Life After Sunday <http://www.lifeaftersunday.com> offers discussion of topical issues and provides information on small-group formation.

Heritage House <http://www.heritagehouse76.com> offers pro-life resources for teachers and adults.

# APPENDIX B

. . . . . . . . . . . .

## What Can I Do to Have Fun and
## Show Affection Without Having Sex?

Here are some creative date ideas.

Visit a zoo, browse a museum, cook together, attend open houses and act interested in buying, color in a coloring book, listen to controversial talk radio and discuss, draw pictures for each other, play in a park, hike, picnic, play washers, go to a conservation area, learn to swing dance together, stargaze, go to the movies, browse a farmer's market, watch airplanes take off and come in (at or near an airport), people-watch at malls or other public places, watch UFOs, drive around and look at houses in ritzy neighborhoods, go roller blading, paint a mural on your bedroom wall, watch TV, tie-dye, look at Christmas lights (during Christmas season, of course), baby-sit together, camp, watch and feed ducks at a park, praise God, watch theater productions—indoor and outdoor, sled in the snow, fish, slowly take a long moonlit walk, play hide and seek, make sock puppets, jump in leaf piles, play basketball, play baseball, climb a tree, volunteer at a soup kitchen, serve the poor, visit a friend, read to each other, drive around the countryside, take a rosary walk, attend church, go on mysterious double dates, visit caves, go creeking, play sports, take an interest in others' activities, do community service, visit a youth group you've never been to, bike, watch a sunrise followed by an outdoor (or campfire) breakfast, play Frisbee golf, pitch horseshoes, make a video, play mud volleyball, clean out a closet together, play children's games, read the newspaper to someone in a nursing home, play board games, imitate animals and try to guess them, play charades, visit a farm (or work at one for a day), window shop, go four-wheeling, visit a Humane Society or pet store to look at animals, visit historic sites, go to the library and read favorite books in the kids section, try different churches, study together at a unique public place, cook a meal for your date, fly a kite, host a game night, wash a car, create a scavenger hunt for each other (to visit "familiar" places and do silly things in public to get clues), plan any random act of kindness, write a story together, write a song together, swim, read a book on dating, relationships, or other interesting topics and discuss them, jog, make a time capsule, walk through old college campuses in the fall, put a jigsaw puzzle together, have a water fight, have a food fight, exercise, attend an aerobics or kick-boxing class, play very competitively at an arcade, rent a video, go bowling, dye your hair, pick apples at a local orchard, eat at a fast-food restaurant, visit a coffeehouse and sip cappuccino, do a project together (for either's family or house), play miniature golf, go grocery shopping, attend a trivia night, go to garage sales and buy weird things for each other or to donate, buy a dozen carnations and randomly give them to people (at the airport you could give them to people getting off the plane with no one waiting to greet them—then say "welcome to _____" or just tell people to have a nice day), go to the dollar movie show, feed each other ice cream, make a cake, play with Play-Doh, plan and go on a day-long road trip, blow bubbles, ice-skate, organize and run fun games for kids at playgrounds, take a horse and carriage ride, make a list of your "favorites" and test their knowledge of how well they know you, go kayaking or canoeing, go to a bookstore and independently pick out books the other would love or should read, throw a party, attend a minor or major league baseball game, go horseback riding, ski, go to a concert, take ballroom dance lessons, plan a dinner out with each course at a different place, organize a float trip, attend a hockey game, go to an amusement park, attend a murder mystery dinner, plan a murder mystery dinner and invite close friends as suspects/victims, go whitewater rafting, attend a retreat.

Here are some creative ways to show that you care.

Tell the other person that you love them, hug, hold hands, give a special gift, be there when they need to talk, spend time together, walk arm in arm in the woods, make a special tape/CD of meaningful or funny or love songs, talk openly about your feelings, share your dreams with each other, snuggle up together, sit together in the park, take a walk together, get to know their friends, send a funny card, plan special meals or days for the other person full of things they'd love, bake their favorite cookies, write letters to each other, take them to their favorite sporting event, respect and honor the other person more than you imagined you could, play footsie, take them to their favorite store, gaze at each other, wash each other's cars, share one "high" and one "low" of each day with each other, use eye contact to share a private thought, send each other care packages with candy or random stuff, dedicate a song on the radio, share lifetime goals with each other, spend time getting to know each other's family, watch a sunset, do a chore for the other, whisper something nice in the other's ear, play their favorite music, be faithful, make sacrifices for each other, hide a love note where they'll find it, give each other cutesie looks, write a poem, choose a special favorite song, hold each other, give a chastity or purity ring, send flowers, plan a candlelight dinner, propose marriage.

These lists have been adapted from two publications: "Creative Dating 101 in St. Louis, MO," published by the members of the Catholic youth group, God's Gang, in Bridgeton, Missouri, 2000, and "101 Ways to Make Love Without Doin' It," courtesy of Iowa high-school students at Washington High School, Washington, Iowa.

# NOTES

1. Zenit News Agency. "Chastity Gaining Respect, Says Papal Household Preacher." Online Posting: December 13, 2002. ZEO2121307. <www.zenit.org/english>

2. Natural law is the philosophical principle that says there are certain objective moral behaviors that can be discovered by looking historically at civilizations. The set of moral behaviors common to most societies make up the natural law. They include such things as lying on principle, murder (not the same as killing), and infanticide.

3. Evert, Jason. *Pure Love*. El Cajon, Calif.: Catholic Answers, 1999. Online <www.catholic.com/chastity/pure_love.asp>.

4. *Catechism of the Catholic Church* (CCC), paragraph 2339. "Chastity includes an *apprenticeship in self-mastery* which is a training in human freedom. The alternative is clear: either man governs his passions and finds peace, or he lets himself be dominated by them and becomes unhappy. 'Man's dignity therefore requires him to act out of conscious and free choice, as moved and drawn in a personal way from within, and not by blind impulses in himself or by mere external constraint. Man gains such dignity when, ridding himself of all slavery to the passions, he presses forward to his goal by freely choosing what is good and, by his diligence and skill, effectively secures for himself the means suited to this end.'"

5. For a great discussion on this point, see C. S. Lewis' *Mere Christianity*. New York: Macmillan, 1943. Revised edition, 1952. pp. 88–95.

6. Bonacci, Mary Beth. "Chastity." July 16, 2002. <www.staycatholic.com/chastity.htm>.

7. The Medical Institute. "The Facts About Human Papilloma Virus." July 16, 2002. <www.medinstitute.org/medical/index.htm>.

8. Peterson, Karen S. "Study Suggests Teen Sex Linked to Depression, Suicide Tries," *USA Today*, June 6, 2003. <www.usatoday.com/news/health/2003-06-03-teen-usat_x.htm>.

9. Harris, Joshua. *Boy Meets Girl: Say Hello to Courtship*. Portland, Ore.: Multnomah Publishers, 2000, p. 151.

10. *"This is my commandment, that you love one another as I have loved you. No one has greater love than this, to lay down one's life for one's friends"* (Jn 15:12–13).

11. John Paul II. "The Holy Father's Second Speech at Kiel Center." Papal Youth Gathering, January 26, 1999, Kiel Center, St. Louis, Missouri. <www.archstl.org/papalvisit/kiel2.htm>.

12. Harris, p. 151.

13. This phrase is borrowed from Mary Beth Bonacci, who may not have coined it, but who uses it regularly in her chastity presentations.

14. Bonacci, Mary Beth. "Love and Sex: What Is the Connection?" 1996. Catholic Educators Resource Center website, July 16, 2002. <http.//catholiceducation.org/articles/sexuality/ se0021.html>.

15. Morris, Desmond. *Intimate Behavior: A Zoologist's Classic Study of Human Intimacy*. New York, Random House, 1971. pp. 74–78, as cited in Donald M. Joy, *Bonding: Relationships in the Image of God*. Waco, Tex.: Word Books, 1985, pp. 41–53. (Parenthetical descriptions and step 12 are author's additions.)

16. Smith, Janet. "Pope Paul VI As Prophet: Have *Humanae Vitae's* Bold Predictions Come True." September 1994. <www.ewtn.com/library/PROLIFE/PPAULPRO.TXT>.

17. Smith, Janet. "Contraception: Why Not." May 1994. Catholic Educator's Resource Center. <www.catholiceducation.org/directory/current_issues/sexuality>.

18. Center for Disease Control and Prevention. "Tracking the Hidden Epidemics: Trends in STDs in the United States 2000." <www.cdc.gov/nchstp/dstd/Stats_Trends/Trends2000.pdf>, p. 2.

19. Food and Drug Administration. "Birth Control Guide." August 2002. <www.fda.gov/fdac/features/1997/babyguide.pdf>.

20. Evert, Jason. *If You Really Loved Me*. Ann Arbor, Mich.: Charis Books, 2003. p. 149. Also, Susan G. Komen Breast Cancer Foundation. "How Hormones Affect Breast Cancer." November 14, 2003. <http://www.komen.org/bci/RiskFactorsAnd Prevention /HowHormonesAffectBreastCancer.asp>.

21. Paul VI, *Humanae Vitae*, paragraph 16.

22. The methods of determining fertility, whether a woman is attempting to conceive or to prevent pregnancy, rely on natural signs. Regular, scientific observation of basal body temperature, vaginal and cervical mucus, and position of the uterus makes determining periods of fertility and infertility reliable.

23. CCC, paragraph 2730.

24. CCC, paragraph 2395.

25. John Paul II. *The Theology of the Body: Human Love in the Divine Plan*. Boston: Pauline Books, 1997.

26. CCC, paragraph 2353.

27. West, Christopher. *Good News About Sex & Marriage*. Ann Arbor, Mich.: Servant Publications, 2000. p. 81.

28. Though we have not touched upon it in depth, this is where the Church's teaching on celibacy takes on meaning. Our natural desire for union mirrors and reflects that union with God which we are all called to by virtue of our baptism. Some people are called to skip the reflection and go straight to the union. Priests and religious live out the union with God that marriage points to. Both aspects are healthy understandings of our sexuality and its purpose in our spirituality.

29. A different genetic influence would be a predisposition to behavior, for example, as is sometimes the case with alcoholism. Those

with alcoholism in their families are not condemned to be drunks, but they may have a stronger tendency toward that behavior than those without the genetic background.

30. Catholic Medical Association. "Homosexuality and Hope." <www.cathmed.org./publications/ homosexuality.html>.

31. As cited in "Homosexuality and Hope."

32. Heft, Jim, S. M., Chancellor and Professor of Faith and Culture at the University of Dayton.

33. The sacrament of reconciliation stems from Jesus' command to the apostles, "*Truly, I tell you, whatever you bind on earth will be bound in heaven, and whatever you loose on earth will be loosed in heaven*" (Mt 18:18, 16:19). Reconciliation completes the healing process that begins with personal repentance. Jesus instituted this sacrament because he understood that humans need to say out loud their failings (as "AA" and altar calls require a verbal or visible step) and they need to hear the words, "you are forgiven," in return.

34. For more, check out the discussion on our thought life in the chapter on "Just My Thoughts" (page 62), and the practical advice in chapters "What to Do" (page 133), "How Can Women Live Chastely" (page 138), and "How Can Men Live Chastely" (page 144).

35. Saint Paul writes: "*Because he himself was tested by what he suffered, he is able to help those who are being tested*" (Heb 2:18) and "*For we do not have a high priest who is unable to sympathize with our weaknesses, but we have one who in every respect has been tested [tempted] as we are, yet without sin*" (Heb 4:15).

36. Billhartz, Cynthia. "Oral Sex Shh." *St. Louis Post-Dispatch*, October 6, 2002. Everyday section, p. E1.

37. Centers for Disease Control and Prevention. "Can I Get HIV From Someone Performing Oral Sex on Me?" January 10, 2003, update. <www.cdc.gov/hiv/pubs/faq/faq20.htm>. Also, Centers

for Disease Control and Prevention. "Can I Get HIV From Performing Oral Sex?" <www.cdc.gov/hiv/pubs/faq/faq19.htm>.
March 31, 2003, update.

38. Visit <www.pureintimacy.com> to find some great resources for
those struggling with pornography or those who love someone
who is struggling with pornography.

39. Evert. *Pure Love.*

40. Evert. *If You Really Loved Me,* p. 87.

41. Read the chapter on "If Not Sex, What Can I Do?" (page 54),
for specific suggestions in creating physical boundaries.